I0163946

THE TABERNACLE

GOD DWELT AMONG MEN

LESLIE M JOHN

THE TABERNACLE

GOD DWELT AMONG MEN

LESLIE M JOHN

My messages are simple thoughts generated in me after reading Bible and various books. My main purpose is evangelism, and not for offending any individual or organization or for discussion by various denominations.

My writings are deposited with Library of Congress Copyright Office, 101 Independence Avenue, SE Washington, DC 20559-6000, USA, and certificates obtained. All Scriptures in electronic format are from King James Version (KJV) from Open domain.

ISBN-10: 0-9890283-6-4

ISBN-13:978-0-9890283-6-3

Table of Contents

PREFACE

I.   My mission is to proclaim the good news of our
       Lord Jesus Christ as revealed to me through Holy
       Bible and from various teachers, preachers, and
       commentators. This is my voluntary service to
       God in the name of His only begotten Son Lord
       Jesus Christ. I share the truth of knowledge of
       God with others with good intention of bringing
       them to the knowledge of the living God, the God
       of Abraham, the God of Isaac, the God of Jacob,
       and the Father of our Lord Jesus Christ.

II.   I pray for the peace of Jerusalem and desire that
       all Jews may accept Lord Jesus as their personal
       Savior and Messiah.

III.   "Pray for the peace of Jerusalem: they shall
       prosper that love thee" (Psalms 122:6)

IV.   There are fundamental truths which I will not
       compromise upon. Explanations, on which
       Christians dispute among themselves, are
       secondary to the fundamental truths that I
       believe in. My mission is not to convert any one
       to Christianity or make any attempt in the
       direction of forcible conversions. One may accept
       or reject any or part of my teachings.

V.   I firmly believe in the saying of Jesus, who said:

       "No man can come to me, except the Father
       which hath sent me draw him: and I will raise
       him up at the last day" John 6:44. My efforts to

teach or preach are of no use unless Jesus Himself intervenes and the Father draws a person unto Jesus

INTRODUCTION

It is so amazing that the Almighty God who created heaven and who cannot be contained in man-made buildings loved man so much that He sent His only begotten Son for our sake. God is a Spirit (John 4:24) and He went before the children of Israel by day in a pillar of a cloud and led them; and he went before them in a pillar of fire by night to give them light. (Exodus 13:21).

The LORD went before the children of Israel in a thick cloud in order that the people may hear when He speaks to Moses. (Exodus 19:9) The LORD dwelt among them unseen by any one, yet performing miracles and helping them. In the Old Testament period God came and dwelt among the children of Israel and in the New Testament period the incarnate God humbled himself and dwelt among men in the form of man.

"And the LORD descended in the cloud, and stood with him there, and proclaimed the name of the LORD". (Exodus 34:5)

"For the cloud of the LORD was upon the tabernacle by day, and fire was on it by night, in the sight of all the house of Israel, throughout all their journeys". (Exodus 40:38)

"But will God indeed dwell on the earth? behold,

the heaven and heaven of heavens cannot contain thee; how much less this house that I have builded?" (1 Kings 8:27)

"And the Word was made flesh, and dwelt among us, (and we beheld his glory, the glory as of the only begotten of the Father,) full of grace and truth". (John 1:14)

"Who, being in the form of God, thought it not robbery to be equal with God: But made himself of no reputation, and took upon him the form of a servant, and was made in the likeness of men: And being found in fashion as a man, he humbled himself, and became obedient unto death, even the death of the cross". (Philippians 2:6-8)

God, who at sundry times and in divers manners spake in time past unto the fathers by the prophets, Hath in these last days spoken unto us by his Son, whom he hath appointed heir of all things, by whom also he made the worlds; Who being the brightness of his glory, and the express image of his person, and upholding all things by the word of his power, when he had by himself purged our sins, sat down on the right hand of the Majesty on high; (Hebrews 1:1-3)

As we are called "Christians" in the New Testament period it is imperative that we should know about the "Tabernacle" and the pattern of the 'Old Covenant' and the 'New Covenant'. Hebrews Chapter 9 provides us knowledge about the contrast between the 'Old Covenant' and the 'New Covenant'.

CHAPTER 1
WHAT IS 'TABERNACLE'?

The word 'Tabernacle' means a portable structure, which was also called the 'Sanctuary', where God came and dwelt among Israelites when they journeyed from Egypt to Canaan. God instructed Moses to build this 'Sanctuary' according to His specifications. God decided the measurements and the elements therein that He may come and dwell therein among His chosen people, the Israelites.

The measurements and the details are specified in Exodus25:8-10. According to Hebrews 9:15 Lord Jesus Christ is the mediator of the New Covenant and by means of His death for the redemption of the transgressions of those saints, who believed in "Yahweh", during Old Testament Period, the promise of eternal inheritance for them was assured. For the New Testament believers also the death of Jesus on the cross of Calvary provided the way for redemption from sin.

The sacrifices offered in the Old Testament period were not enough for them to have redemption from their sins, but those sacrifices were the assurances of their future redemption through the blood of Lord Jesus shed for everyone. A Testament comes into effect after the death of the testator. "For where a testament is, there must also of necessity be the death of the testator". (Hebrews 9:16)

It is worth knowing the composition of ourselves. Man is composed of three parts -- the BODY, the SOUL, and the SPIRIT. [Man in general includes men and women.] Body is the physical structure of the man. Lord Jesus and Apostle Paul referred to the Body as the "flesh" in several references in the New Testament. This is the outer most part of man. The body in general perishes but the body of the born-again child in specific acquires glorified body when Lord Jesus Christ comes again. (Ref: 1 Cor. 15:38-40; 1 Thess. 4:14-17).

Soul is the immaterial part of a person; the actuating cause of an individual life. It does not consist of matter and it is incorporeal that is it does not have a body or form. This is the inner self of human, the very man with thoughts. The soul never perishes. The Soul of born-again child of God will be with the Lord Jesus Christ always.

The Soul of the unsaved man will be cast into hell and later into lake of fire for suffering for ever and ever. The souls of the saved ones are comforted in Paradise in the third heaven until the time of second coming of Jesus Christ. They stand before the judgment seat of Christ in the mid-air and receive their rewards for their good works. The Soul of the born-again child will be with the Lord instantly when he dies.

Luke 23:43 reads "And Jesus said unto him, Verily I say unto thee, To day shalt thou be with me in paradise".

The Soul of the unsaved one will remain in the hell and tormented until the time of final judgment and they will be judged at the great white throne. They along with Satan and his fallen angels, death and hell will be cast in to the lake fire. [Rev.19:20, 20:10, 20:14, 15]

The Spirit is the breath of life given by God. God breathed His spirit into the nostrils of man when he created him; so the spirit of saved or unsaved will return to God. The Spirit of a person never dies. God, who gives spirit, takes it back to him in his own time.

It is so interesting to see that the Tabernacle also has three parts -- the Outer, the Inner, which is the "Holy Place" and the inner most, which is the "Most Holy". It is at the "Most Holy Place" that God Spoke to the high priest. It is at this "Most Holy place" that Lord Jesus entered with His own blood to give access for believers in Him to worship The Father.

The curtain of the Temple was rent from top to bottom, without any human intervention, revealing to us that all believers have access to the Father with the only mediator, who is our

Lord Jesus Christ.

The first covenant had ordinances of divine services offered in the tabernacle, which was made of several elements namely,

IN THE OUTER COURT

1. *Brazen Altar*
2. *The Laver*

IN THE HOLY PLACE

1. *Candlestick (i.e. Seven-Stick Lampstand [Menorah])*
2. *The table and the Shewbread*
3. *The Golden Censer (The Golden Altar)*

IN THE MOST HOLY PLACE

1. *Ark of the Covenant.*

THE BRASEN ALTAR – DESCRIPTION

(Also called The Bronze Altar)

There were two Altars in the Tabernacle – One immediately near the gate, where the sacrifices are made: this was the 'Brazen Altar' and the second Altar was made of Gold and was placed inside the holy place, where the priest offered incense. This Golden Altar was not inside the 'most holy place' but inside the curtains, which were the first veil.

The New Testament sets a new pattern of worship for the children of God in order to give the finest recognition of the God in Trinity, the Father, the Son and the Holy Spirit. The writer of Hebrews in Chapter 13:9-16 refers to the strange doctrines being spread among Christians about the necessity of a priest, eating certain kinds of foods, offerings and the sacrifices at the sanctuary.

Ceremonial rites such as restriction to certain types of foods constrain the approach to the Father in Heaven, through His one and Only Son, Jesus Christ. Altar is the place on which sacrifices are offered as a token of atonement of sins.

The Altar is outside the 'most holy place', where the "Ark of Covenant" is placed. The Altar is the place, where our sins are cleansed and we are no more there but in the most Holy Place, which is open to all of us, through the blood of Jesus Christ shed upon the cross of Calvary, and when the veil of the temple was torn from top to the bottom without any human intervention.

It is the divine access given to the New Testament believer through our High Priest, Lord Jesus Christ, who became atoning sacrifice for us.

Jesus yielded His spirit into the hands of the Father in heaven with a loud voice crying, "It is finished", and "Father, into your hands I commend my spirit: and having said this, he gave up the spirit" (Luke 23:46).

Jesus accomplished the mission on which He was, while He was here on this earth. His mission was to take up your sins and my sins upon Himself and die for our sake on the Altar. He became our Altar, and He became our High Priest, and He became our Perfect Tabernacle. There is no fear for us to speak to the Father in heaven through Jesus Christ, who alone is the mediator for us.

There is no priest or any human mediator required for us to speak to the Father in heaven. Let us introspect here, as to whether we are still standing at the Brazen Altar or are we entering the place where the God is speaking to us from the 'mercy seat'. Let us approach the Father in heaven through the only mediator, Lord Jesus Christ, who is now seated on the right hand of the Majesty and pleading on behalf of us, and upholding us blameless.

THE LAVER - DESCRIPTION

Located between the Bronze Altar and the Golden Altar was the 'Laver'. The Bronze Altar was outside the Holy Place while the Golden

Altar was inside the 'Holy Place'. The priest had to wash his hands and legs with the water taken out from the laver before entering into the Holy Place to perform the ceremonial rites related to the 'Holy Place' and the 'Most Holy Place'. The Bronze Altar was the place where the sacrifices were offered and the Golden Altar was the place where incense was offered.

The LORD spoke to Moses and said to him that a laver of brass be made and located between the Bronze Altar where the congregation gather and the Golden Altar where incense is offered. The priest may enter the 'Holy Place' only after washing his hands and legs with the water taken out from this laver.

The foot of the 'laver' was to be made of brass and of the looking-glasses of the women, who assembled at the door of the tabernacle. The looking-glasses of women signified the religious devotion of the woman and the woman participated in this religious tradition with great zeal. The instructions were that the laver should contain water. Aaron and his sons needed to cleanse their hands and feet at the 'laver' so that they may not die.

The washing was necessary before they go near the Golden Altar to minister. They needed to burn the offering made by fire unto the LORD. The instructions from the LORD were so severe that if they did not wash their hands and feet before entering into the 'Holy Place' to burn the offering made by fire unto the LORD they will die, and these instructions were given unto them and to generation to come from his seed. (Ex. 30:17-21; 38:8 and 40:30).

Moses obeyed the LORD and conveyed to the congregation the words of the LORD and then brought Aaron and his sons and washed them with water. (Lev. 8:5-6)

The Psalmist in Psalm 119:9 says, "Wherewithal shall a young man cleanse his way? by taking heed thereto according to thy word". Christ loved the Church. Apostle Paul exhorts that husbands should love their wives just as Christ loved the Church, which is His bride.

The believers in Christ need to wash themselves before the Lord every day of their sins so that He may sanctify and wash the Assembly (Ekklesia) and present it as glorious entity, pure and holy, without any blemish or wrinkle. (Ephesians 5:25-27).

The necessity of cleansing by the believer in Christ does not give him a license to sin every day and confess of his/her sin as a routine, but the necessity is to live a holy life throughout one's life period, until he/she leaves this world, lest it should mean that the believer is crucifying Jesus every day. This does not mean that God will not pardon the sins of the believer, who may willfully commit in his/her daily life, but it emphasizes the need to remain holy unto the Lord.

If the believer in Christ sins, he/she will certainly lose the rewards in heaven, to the extent that he sinned and as the Lord may decide at His discretion.

The believer is at risk of losing the grace of the Lord, whom he crucifies daily in his/her life. In the Old Testament period whenever there was a trespass of the law he/she died or was put to death under two or three witnesses.

Salvation once gained will never be lost but if any believer renounces the Lord fully and tramples the Son of God, despising the blood of the Lord and his new covenant under which the believer is saved and in addition despise the spirit of grace the consequences are very serious. (Hebrews 10:25-30)

The need for washing from the water of the laver before entering the 'Holy Place' signifies that the dwelling of the LORD in the tabernacle consecrates the place as holy.

"In the beginning was the Word, and the Word was with God, and the Word was God. (John 1:1)"

The Word was made flesh and dwelt among us and believer's body is a holy temple for the Lord to dwell. John testifies that the Word dwelt among us and we beheld His glory, the glory of the only begotten of the Father in heaven. The Word was full of grace and truth. The Word is our Lord, and He is Jesus, our savior. The children of Israel sang a song unto the LORD, when He delivered from the bondage of slavery under Pharaoh.

The song of Moses (Exodus 15:1-10) exalts the name of the LORD, who delivered from them from slavery and triumphant gloriously. He was their strength and song and He became their salvation and their God.

The LORD is the LORD of wars and He had cast Pharaoh's chariots and his host in to the Red Sea. The enemy pursued them but could not prevail. Pharaoh and his army were drowned in the Red Sea.

Recounting these facts John in his vision as recorded in Revelation 15:2-3 says that he saw a sea of glass mingled with fire and those, who got victory over the beast and his image and his mark, and over his number of his name, and they stood on the sea of glass, having the harps of God and they sang the song of Moses unto the Lamb of God, saying His works are marvelous and the Lord God Almighty was His name.

Innocent as he was, the most loved disciple of Jesus, Peter did not know the importance of washing of feet by the Lord. Jesus washed the feet of his disciples and taught them as to how to humble oneself and minister to become worthy of the Lord. Peter asked Jesus as to why he was washing their feet and wipe them with the towel, which he used for girding him. Peter was about to refuse to accept the ministry of Jesus when he attempted to wash his feet, but then Jesus said to him, that if he did not allow Jesus to wash his feet, he had no part with Him. Peter then prayed to Jesus that He may wash not only his feet but also his hands and head. Jesus in turn said to him that he that is already washed needed no full bath but only cleansing (John 13:5-10).

Every branch that is in Jesus bears fruit and Jesus purges the branch that keeps bearing fruit for him, so that the branch may bring forth more fruit. Jesus cleanses us from our sins every day and makes us worthy to be presented as holy ones before the Majesty in heaven. (John 13:5-10 and 15:2-3).

It is the love of God that made Him to send His only begotten Son into this world so that we may be saved. Christ died for us even when we were in sin and were justified by His blood and were saved from the wrath through Him. We were His enemies, but though Jesus we are reconciled unto the Father in heaven. (Romans 5:8-10). Therefore, Jesus gave unto the disciples the power to go into the nations and preach the gospel and assured them that He will be with them always.

Speaking to the Samaritan woman Jesus said, "But whosoever drinketh of the water that I shall give him shall never thirst; but the water that I shall give him shall be in him a well of water springing up into everlasting life". (John 4:14).

It emphasizes the need to purify our souls and to obey the Word of God, the truth through the Holy Spirit, so that brethren may love one another with pure hearth fervently. (1 Peter 1:22)

THE "CANDLESTICK" - DESCRIPTION
[Also called "lampstand" or "Menorah"]

The God of Abraham, Isaac, and Jacob, whose name is the "God Almighty", and, who called Himself by the name "JEHOVAH" (Exodus: 6:3) led the children of Israel through the wilderness unto the land of Canaan, the promised land flowing with milk and honey.

In their journey from Egypt to Canaan after redeeming them from the bondage of slavery under Pharaoh, the LORD spoke to Moses many times and gave several instructions to him to lead the children of Israel. The LORD spoke to Moses very clearly about the construction of the "Tabernacle" in a specified way to the measurements He desired to have. In the Tabernacle the elements were placed at certain places as the LORD told Moses.

The "Candlestick" was made of pure gold that was hammered out skillfully with its shaft, its branches, its bowls, its knobs, and its flowers, to stand on one piece. Six branches of lamps; three on either side of the center piece stood elegantly on one piece above the shaft. The seven lamps were to be kept burning always never to get extinguished. Moses made the "lampstand" just as the LORD commanded him to do.

"Three bowls made after the fashion of almonds in one branch, a knop and a flower; and three bowls made like almonds in another branch, a knop and a flower: so throughout the six branches going out of the candlestick". (Exodus 37:19)

The candlestick was placed near the veil inside the holy place before entering the "most holy place" and this was the sole light inside the tent. This candlestick with its seven branches gave light to the whole area inside the tent. This is same as the seven lamps of fire before burning before the throne, as John saw in Revelation CHAPTER 4:5.

The seven lamps were the seven Spirits of God. When John wrote to the seven churches in Asia, he greeted them saying, "... Grace be unto you, and peace, from him who is, and who was, and who is to come; and from the seven Spirits who are before his throne; (Revelation 1:4)"

It is hard for natural man to perceive these things but for those led by the Spirit of God these facts are clearly let known by the LORD. For others, these facts appear as "foolishness" (1 Corinthians 2:14-15). In Jesus was life and that life was the light of men (John 1:4), and when this light shone in darkness, the darkness comprehended it not, but "Christ became a high priest of good things to come, by a greater and more perfect tabernacle, not made with hands..." Hebrews 9:11). Jesus said that He is the light of the world and whoever follows him shall not walk in darkness, but shall have the light of life. (John 8:12).

Prophet Malachi prophesied about Jesus and called him as "The Sun of righteousness". Indeed, Jesus is greater light than the two great lights, the sun, the moon, and the stars that he created one to rule the day, and others to rule the night respectively. Pharisees alleged him that Jesus bore a wrong record of Him, and said that the record was not true.

Jesus replied to them that they perceived Him not rightly for if they perceived him rightly they would have known who the Father in heaven is and who he is. In John 10:30 Jesus asserted that He and The Father are one. The LORD instructed Moses to command the children of Israel that they should bring pure olive oil for the light to burn always in the Tabernacle and that shall be a statute for the children of Israel unto generations forever.

Whoever believes that Jesus is the Son of God and whoever loves Him becomes the spiritual child of God. In God is the light and there is no darkness at all. If we say that we have fellowship with Him, we will not walk in darkness, but if we walk in darkness we lie and if we walk in the light we have fellowship with one another and the blood of Jesus Christ cleanses us from all our sin (1 John 1:5-7)

The LORD instructed Moses that the golden "lampstand" shall be placed before the veil by the ark of the testimony before the mercy seat. It is at this place, that the LORD said, he would meet Moses. There were three pieces of furniture in the Holy place, which was the first portion of the tent. The "most holy place" was the second portion of the tent that had the "Ark of the Covenant".

The three pieces of furniture were in the "Holy Place" and they were: (1) "The golden "lampstand ""also called, "Menorah" or "Candlestick", (2) "The table of showbread" and (3) "The golden altar of incense".

The LORD instructed Moses that Aaron shall burn sweet incense every morning when he dresses up the lamps and he shall light the lamps every evening as well. The LORD called it as the "perpetual incense" before Him for generations. The perpetual burning of the incense on the Golden Altar and lighting of the lamps lets us know the love of Christ, who intercedes perpetually on behalf of us with the Majesty in heaven. We are exhorted in Hebrews 13:15 that we should offer the sacrifice of praise to God continually. It is the fruit of our lips giving thanks to His name. The LORD prohibited offering of any strange incense before Him. The LORD was very serious and particular about the worship in a specified way.

When Nadab and Abihu, the sons of Aaron made a mistake in burning incense, the fire of the LORD devoured them. Nadab and Abihu did something that God did not command them; each one of them took a censer each, put fire therein, and put incense thereon and offered strange fire before the Lord. That offering of strange fire before the Lord resulted in their death. (Leviticus 10:1-3). This shows us that God does not like religious practices and traditions but He is pleased with the only kind of worship that He wants in His own way.

God is against those, who divide Christians in the name of Paul, and Apollos, Cephas etc. (1 Corinthians 1:11-13) Christ is not divided nor was Paul crucified for anyone and none is baptized in the name of Paul. Let none judge us in meat or in drink or on any holyday, or the new moon, or of Sabbath days, nor does any should misguide us that worshipping angels fetches us some reward. (Colossians 2:16-19)

Jesus said, "As long as I am in the world, I am the light of the world. (John 9:5)" and in the "Sermon on the mount" Jesus said, "Ye are the salt of the earth: but if the salt has lost his savor, wherewith shall it be salted? it is thenceforth good for nothing, but to be cast out, and to be trodden under foot of men. Ye are the light of the world. A city that is set on a hill cannot be hid". (Matthew 5:13-14).

THE TABLE AND THE SHEWBREAD - DESCRIPTION

The Lord Jesus Christ on the night when He was betrayed instituted the Lord's Supper in order that His death upon the cross of Calvary for the remission of our sins may be remembered by those, who have accepted Him as personal Savior.

The Scriptures exhort us that this participation in the Lord's Supper should be done as often as possible in remembrance of Lord Jesus Christ's death. In Matthew 26:26-30 there is a description of the Lord's Supper and this was made clear by Apostle Paul in his Epistle to 1 Corinthians 11:23-29.

On the first day of the week, when the disciples

came together they broke bread in remembrance of the Lord's death. (Acts 20:7) In the Old Testament a shadow of this Lord Table was seen in Exodus Chapter 25:23-30; 37:10-16 and Leviticus 24:5-9

The LORD spoke to Moses and gave instruction to him that in the Tabernacle he shall place a table of shittim wood, the length of which should be two cubits, the breadth of which should be a cubit and the height of which should be a cubit and half. The LORD also told Moses that he should overlay the table with pure gold and "and make thereto a crown of gold round about". The detailed instructions are given in Exodus Chapter 25-23-30 and these instructions were carried out by Moses as we can read in Chapter 37:10-16.

The LORD told Moses that the showbread should always be set before Him. This showbread should be of fine flour, twelve cakes baked and each of the baked cake shall have two tenth deals. The two tenth deals are equivalent to two omers and each omer is equivalent to the tenth part of an ephah, which is about five gallons. (Exodus 16:3 and International Standard Bible Encyclopedia).

The twelve cakes set in two rows of six each upon the pure table before the LORD represent the twelve tribes of Israel, whom God will remember always in compliance with His own everlasting covenant that He made with Israel. The LORD instructed that pure frankincense shall be put on each row, and the bread shall be a memorial even an offering made by fire unto the LORD. The Lord's instructions were that the table of showbread be set in order every Sabbath continually that the LORD may remember His own everlasting covenant with Israel. The LORD instructed that Aaron and his sons that they should eat the showbread in the holy place because it was the most holy of all the offerings that were made before the LORD by fire and that shall be a perpetual statute. (Leviticus 24:5-9).

A New Testament believer in Christ is not asked to be legalistic about the number of breads, the type of bread, and the measurements of the table or of the bread. The New Testament believer is the one who is washed in the blood of Jesus Christ; whether it is Jew or Gentile. Every saved child of God is a member of the Church, which is His bride.

The Church is above Jew or Gentile and the privileges, blessings and the promises given to the Church are great even above the ones who are Jews. New Testament believer is also asked not to observe days, months and seasons. Let us be careful of knowing that the bread and wine given at the Lord's Supper do not turn into real body and real blood of Jesus as the belief "Transubstantiation" says, but the bread and the wine are nothing more than emblems representing the body of Jesus and the blood of Jesus. We do remember Lord's death until He comes by breaking the bread and eating from it and drinking from the cup.

Lord Jesus took upon Himself the iniquities of mankind and was crucified upon the cross of Calvary. He took the position that was lesser than that of angels for the sake of suffering upon the cross in order that you and I may have everlasting life. He was crowned with glory and honor.

Before going to the cross Jesus instituted the Table and amidst the twelve disciples He broke the bread and said, "Take, eat, this is my body", and asked them to do in remembrance of His death. He had earlier stated that Moses gave them the bread but it was not from heaven, but the bread that Jesus gave was from the Father in heaven and it was the true bread that is available for all of us.

The bread that Jesus gave to us is from heaven. When the disciples asked them the bread of life, perhaps they thought that it is for living a daily life, but Jesus told them that He Himself is the bread of life, and whoever goes to him shall never hunger and whoever believe in Him shall never thirst. (John 6:32-35).

Reminding the disciples that the bread that the Israelites ate in the wilderness was "manna" and they died of natural death, but whoever eats the bread of life, which is in Jesus Himself shall never hunger nor will thirst. He is the living bread and came down from heaven and whoever tastes Him shall be blessed with the partaking in His flesh and "will give the life of the world". (John 6:48-51)

Therefore, Jesus stands always at the door of sinner's heart and knocks ceaselessly to open his heart in order that He may enter therein and dwell in his heart and to sup with him. The Lord asked John to write to the angel of the church of the Laodicea's that they were lukewarm and God will spew them out of His mouth. God desired that they be either hot or cold.

"Behold, I stand at the door, and knock: if any man hear my voice, and open the door, I will come in to him, and will sup with him, and he with me". (Revelation 3:20)

Emphasizing the need of the Lord's supper Apostle Paul writes in 1 Corinthians 11:23-29 as follows:

"For I have received of the Lord that which also I delivered unto you, That the Lord Jesus the same night in which he was betrayed took bread: And when he had given thanks, he break it, and said, Take, eat: this is my body, which is broken for you: this do in remembrance of me. After the same manner also he took the cup, when he had supped, saying, This cup is the new testament in my blood: this do ye, as oft as ye drink it, in remembrance of me. For as often as ye eat this bread, and drink this cup, ye do shew the Lord's death till he come. Wherefore whosoever shall eat this bread, and drink this cup of the Lord, unworthily, shall be guilty of the body and blood of the Lord. But let a man examine himself, and so let him eat of that bread, and drink of that cup. For he that eateth and drinketh unworthily, eateth and drinketh damnation to himself, not discerning the Lord's body"

THE GOLDEN ALTAR - DESCRIPTION
(Also called the Altar of Incense)

The description and the measurements of the Golden Altar and the restrictions in offering strange fire are described in Exodus 30:1-10. The sweet spices that God liked were 'stacte', 'onycha' and 'galbanum'. These sweet spices with pure frankincense were pleasing to the LORD. Moses did everything just as God commanded and the golden altar was set before the ark of the testimony.

Priest Zachariah had to perform a duty in the course of his legal turn a service which was to burn the incense in the temple of the Lord. There was a multitude of people who stood outside the temple when he went into the temple to perform the service.

In Luke 1st Chapter we read that the angel of the Lord, Gabriel, appeared to Zachariah on the right side of the altar to announce that he would have a child, who upon growing, would 'prepare a way' for the Lord Jesus to come into the world to save sinners.

The incense offered at the right place brought positive and pleasing answer coming from the Lord. In Contrast we see in the Old Testament Nadab and Abihu, who were the sons of chosen priest Aaron making great mistake in offering incense and they reaped severe punishment from the Lord.

Each one of them took his censer and put fire therein, and put incense thereon, and offered strange fire before the LORD. They were in violation of offering strange fire before the LORD. The LORD did not command them to do so. The consequence of their own willful action resulted in The LORD pouring out His anger on them.

The fire from the LORD went out from Him and devoured them and they died before LORD. (Leviticus 10:1-2)

Incense is the pleasant odor emitted from the spices when they are burnt. It is the perfume exhaled and, as we read in Old Testament, God liked such pleasant odor from the specified spices in a specific way prescribed by Him. The burning of the spices was to be done at the Golden Altar.

Any violation of His specific instructions resulted in serious consequences even unto death of the one that burnt such incense. The priest's role in burning such incense at a specified place was very important one to take note of.

The Golden Altar was the place upon which such incense was offered in the Tabernacle. A pleasant smoke was emitted from out of the burnt spices, and that smoke went up the chimney into the air and it soared high in to the air.

Revelation 8:4 describes that "the smoke went up with the prayers of saints out of the hand of the angel before God". The soaring smoke before the Lord indicates the acceptance of the prayers from the saints by God. The answer from God is seen when the angel of the Lord takes the censer filled with fire and throws it down on to the earth to destroy the enemies of the Lord Jesus Christ.

No one, who is against the Lord, will escape the severe judgments that God will execute in the last days. Our filthy attitude, filthy thoughts, and filthy behavior are equivalent to the 'strange fire' before the Lord. Let us cleanse ourselves of that filthiness before we offer our incense of prayers to the Lord, so that we may not face chastisement from Him for the filthiness we have in our hearts.

Let us cleanse ourselves of the sins and of that filthiness so that He may bless us. Presence of sin in our heart will result in our prayers not crossing beyond the roof top of our homes; nay they may not even step out beyond the place from where they are offered. Let us have God in our hearts and let us be holy so that He may dwell in our hearts. Our bodies are the temple of God, and if we keep our hearts pure and clean then our hearts will be pleasant place for God to dwell. His dwelling in our hearts will bring joy to us and we will rejoice in the Lord. The Lord said that He will give His peace to us and not the peace that the world gives us.

The Psalmist prayed to God that his prayer be set forth before Him as incense. The writer of the Hebrews asks us to offer the sacrifice of praise to God through our High priest, Lord Jesus Christ, not in the way Jewish priests offered their prayers and incense with all the restrictions seen in the Old Testament, but just as freely as any child could speak to its parent. Our mediator is Lord Jesus Christ and He stands on behalf of us to present our prayers to the Father in heaven and intercedes continually.

There were generations of priests. The priesthood lasted in the Old Testament days, but such priesthood ended when Lord Jesus Christ became our High Priest. He does not belong to the lineage of priests, but He was after the order of Melchisedec (Hebrews 5:6). He offered sacrifice of His own body upon the cross bearing upon Himself, our sins to become a perfect Tabernacle for us and the only High Priest and mediator for us to have communion with the Father in heaven.

"For there is one God, and one mediator between God and men, the man Christ Jesus; who gave himself a ransom for all, to be testified in due time". (1Timothy 2:5-6).

That is our Lord Jesus, the Lamb of God, who took away our sins and washed in His blood. John saw Him on the throne when the Lord took the book; the four beasts and twenty four elders, "having every one of them harps, and golden vials full of odors, which are the prayers of saints" fell down and laid down their crowns before Him.

At the Golden Altar the incense was offered. They were the prayers from the designated priests on behalf of the people to the Lord. We see great prayers and intercessions by two individuals in Scriptures. While Moses intervened on behalf of the children of Israel, we have Lord Jesus Christ intervening not only for those who killed him but also for his disciples.

When Moses and Aaron went into the Tabernacle and came out and blessed the people the glory of the Lord appeared to all the people

"And Moses and Aaron went into the tabernacle of the congregation, and came out, and blessed the people: and the glory of the LORD appeared unto all the people". (Leviticus 9:23)

The consuming of the burnt offering and the fat upon the altar is a sign of acceptance of the Offering by the Lord. When people saw this they shouted and fell on their faces.

"And there came a fire out from before the LORD, and consumed upon the altar the burnt offering and the fat: which when all the people saw, they shouted, and fell on their faces". (Leviticus 9:24)

THE ARK OF THE TESTIMONY - DESCRIPTION
(Also called the 'Ark of the Covenant')

In the most Holy place was the Ark of the Covenant, which was like a box that was made of 'shittim wood' overlaid with pure gold inside and outside. It had staves fixed parallel one to another on either side of the box.

There were four rings of gold on the four corners; two rings on one side and other two rings on the other side. Staves were made of shittim wood and the rings supported the staves and the staves supported the box and this arrangement facilitated the priests to carry the Ark of the Testimony on their shoulders from one place to another. Only priests were allowed to carry the 'Ark of the Covenant; and as we read in the latter books such as 2 Samuel 6:7 the anger of the LORD was killed against Uzzah, and God smote him to death for his error. No one, except the high priest was allowed to go into the most holy place. God told Moses that the Testimony that He gave shall be put in the ark. The Ark of the Testimony had Mercy seat, the Cherubims on it and Aaron's rod that budded, a pot of 'Manna' and the 'Ten Commandments'.

MERCY SEAT

The LORD spoke to Moses and said to him that he should make a 'mercy seat' of pure gold according to the measurements that He specified. The Lord said that the length of the 'mercy seat' should be two cubits, which in modern measurement is equivalent to the length of two fore-arms from the elbow to the tip of the middle finger, probably about 92 inches and its width should be a cubit and half, which is equivalent to probably 69 inches (The measurements in modern terms are disputed and may vary a little bit)

THE CHERUBIMS

The LORD spoke to Moses and said to him that he should make cherubims [(plural of 'Chrerub'), (cherubims are an order of angels)] of gold of beaten work and place them on two ends of the 'mercy seat', so that the cherubims face one toward the other, looking one to another toward the 'mercy seat', with their wings stretched forth on high covering the 'mercy seat'. (Exodus 25:17, 18, 19, 20)

PLACEMENT OF THE 'MERCY SEAT'

The LORD spoke to Moses and said that the 'mercy seat' shall be placed between the two cherubims above upon the ark, and that he should place, in the ark, the testimony that the LORD would give. The LORD said that he will meet Moses and commune with him from above the mercy seat. In His communication from this chosen place of the Lord, He said He would give commandments unto the children of Israel.

The Lord's instruction to Moses about the placement of 'mercy seat' is very specific. According to His instructions the 'mercy seat' shall be put upon the ark of the testimony in the most holy place of the Tabernacle. Moses obeyed the LORD and did just as He instructed. The "mercy seat' was a covering on the 'ark of the testimony', and it was a propitiatory covering, a type of Christ, who became the propitiation of our sins and covered our sins; thus fulfilling the law unto our righteousness.

(Exodus 25:21, 22, 34; Exodus 37:6; Exodus 37:7, 8, 9, Exodus 39:35. Exodus 40:20)

There was the Ark of the Covenant, which was made of 'shittim wood' overlaid with pure gold inside and outside. It had four rings of gold on the four corners; two rings on one side and other two rings on the other side. Staves made of shittim wood were put in the rings by the sides of the ark to facilitate the priests to carry it on their shoulders. God told Moses that the Testimony that He gives shall be put in the ark.

The Mercy Seat of pure gold was made and put upon the ark. Two Cherubims of gold were placed on the ark. One Cherub facing the other and both these Cherubims were placed with their wings stretched covering the Mercy Seat. The Testimony, which God asked Moses to put inside Ark, consisted of:

AARON'S ROD THAT BUDDED

THE TWO TABLETS OF THE TEN COMMANDMENTS

A POT OF MANNA

The details of the measurements of the Ark of the Covenant are mentioned in Exodus Chapter 25. These elements were made the part of the final elements in the temple at Jerusalem.

AARON'S ROD THAT BUDDED

Numbers 16 and 17th Chapters give us the details as to how God chose Aaron for his service. Korah, Dathan, Abiram, the sons of Eliab, On, and the sons of Reuben challenged Moses and his leadership. They murmured against God, and cast allegations against Moses saying that he brought them out from the land of milk and honey, which according to them was Egypt. It is in Egypt where they served as slaves for several years, yet they now call that it was a land of milk and honey. God called Canaan as the land flowing with milk and honey and He was leading them from Egypt to Canaan with Moses as their leader.

However, Korah, Dathan, Abiram and sons of Eliaab, On, and the sons of Reuben alleged that Moses took upper hand and did not give them any important role in the service of God. They did not realize that it is the prerogative of God to choose unto Himself those, who, He thinks are fit for His service and allots to each one according to his ability and sincerity, their portion of service. Moses was chosen to lead the children of Israel, and, Aaron, who was older than Moses was appointed to assist him.

God is angry on those who feel ashamed or afraid of serving him. In such circumstances God may allow someone else to be our aide or speak on behalf of us. When God allows such things to come in our lives we should accept them without any reluctance.

In 1 Corinthians 12:15-26 Apostle Paul writes that each member of the body is important in its own place. One of the many questions he asks is "if the whole body were an eye, where were the hearing". That is to say God chooses every believer to work for him as he desires not as we desire. Everyone can not be a leader in the Church.

Disturbed by the protests of those men, Moses rises in anger and says that God will show by the next day, as to who was chosen by God to lead the children of Israel, and who was not. Moses then orders the protesters and asks them to take censers (censer is something like a fry-pan that was used to carry fire to burn incense before the LORD). Moses said it is not a small thing that God chose certain ones unto Himself for His service in the Tabernacle. Dathan, Abiram and sons of Eliab refuse to come to Moses saying that he brought them from the land of milk and honey, where they had good life.

Slavery under Pharaoh, and the land, where they were slaves was pleasant to them now, even as God was leading them to the real land of milk and honey, which He promised to the children of Israel.

At this point of time, Moses approached the LORD and said to Him that he had not taken even a donkey from them nor did he hurt any one of them. Now, again Moses asks Korah and all his company to stand before the LORD, along with Aaron, the next day. Moses asks them to take every man his censer and put incense in them, put fire in it and bring before the LORD. Every man brought his censer and thus two hundred censers were before the LORD. He asks Aaron also to bring his censer and put fire in it. Everyone gathered at the door of the tabernacle and the glory of the LORD appeared unto the entire congregation.

The LORD spoke to Moses and Aaron and asked them to separate themselves from the congregation, so that He may consume the protesters. At the instructions from the LORD everyone separated from Korah, Dathan, and Abiram.

Moses said to them that if they died of natural death, then it is an indication that Moses was not chosen by God, but if the earth swallowed them by opening its mouth, then it is an indication that God chose Moses to do the service for Him. As they were speaking the earth opened her mouth and swallowed all the protesters and Korah and his goods. There came out a fire from the LORD and consumed two hundred and fifty men who offered incense and God did not like that incense offering.

That was how God showed to the children of Israel that He chose Aaron and his seed alone to come near to offer incense before the LORD. The

LORD showed to them Aaron was not like Korah and his company in serving the LORD. The choosing of Aaron and his seed came to be known through Moses. But, the children of Israel murmured against Moses the very next day again saying that he killed the people of the LORD. As they were speaking the cloud covered and the glory of the LORD again appeared. The LORD was so angry against them He asked Moses to get away from them in order that he may consume them. In order to appease the LORD Moses instructed Aaron to take his censer, put fire in it from off the altar, and put incense and go quickly and make atonement for them.

Aaron did as Moses commanded and ran into the midst of the congregation, and put incense and made atonement for the people. By then the anger of the LORD had already kindled and the plague had begun. Aaron stood between the dead and the living and the plague stopped. But by then fourteen thousand and seven hundred were already killed. This was in addition to the number of people, who died along with Korah. Aaron returned to Moses near the door of the tabernacle and then the plague stopped completely.

God gave them a specific sign at this time that He chose Aaron to do service for Him. The LORD said to Moses to instruct the children of Israel that every one of them may take a rod each according the house of their fathers, in all, twelve rods and then everyone should write his name upon the rod that he took for this purpose. God asked Moses to write the name of Aaron on the rod of Levi and lay all the rods in the tabernacle. God said He will meet Moses in the tabernacle and show that the rod of the one, whom, God has chosen. The LORD said that the rod of the one whom God has chosen will bud and that should be considered as a sign to indicate God's choice. That sign was to bring an end to the murmurings among the children of Israel who were fighting for the leadership in the house of the God. Moses spoke to the children of Israel and asked them to do just as the LORD commanded. They all obeyed and wrote down their names according to their tribes and placed them before the LORD at the tabernacle.

The LORD showed a clear sign there that He has accepted the leadership of Aaron as the priest, who would be performing the duties of priest in offering the prayers and atonement for the children of Israel. While all the rods with the names of those tribes, who presented them to be placed in the tabernacle, remained without having undergone any change, Aaron's rod bore great testimony. The rod of Aaron budded and blossomed.

"...behold, the rod of Aaron for the house of Levi was budded, and brought forth buds, and bloomed blossoms, and yielded almonds..." (Numbers 17:8)

The LORD ordered that this rod of Aaron be kept as testimony in the 'Ark of the covenant', so that the future generations would know that God has chosen Aaron to be the priest. This rod of Aaron had later swallowed the serpents of the magicians. These magicians also made their rods as serpents under the instructions of Pharaoh who tried to undermine the authority of Aaron. But, the serpents of Aaron swallowed the serpents of magicians showing clearly that God is greater than his enemy. In Hebrews 9:4 the writer of Hebrews wrote about the rod of Aaron that budded.

A POT OF MANNA

Moses said to Aaron that the LORD commanded him to tell Aaron that a pot of 'Manna' is kept in the "Ark of the covenant". And Moses said unto Aaron, Take a pot, and put an omer full of manna therein, and lay it up before the LORD, to be kept for your generations. As the LORD commanded Moses, so Aaron laid it up before the Testimony, to be kept. (Exodus 16:33-34) The writer of the Hebrews refers to this in Hebrews 9:4 to show us the importance of the Lord's love and care of His children.

"Which had the golden censer, and the ark of the covenant overlaid round about with gold, wherein was the golden pot that had manna, and Aaron's rod that budded, and the tables of the covenant". (Hebrews 9:4)

This is for everyone to take note of, and remember for generations that the love of the Lord is everlasting and He desired that His love be remembered always.

It is worth knowing some details about 'Manna' and why God instructed Moses that a Pot of Manna be kept in the Ark of the Covenant?

First let us see what is Manna?

The simplest answer is IT WAS THE HEAVENLY BREAD given to the children of Israel when they were on their way from Egypt to Canaan.

The children of Israel had sweet water from God at Marah and rest at Elim. After that, they resumed their journey and reached the wilderness of Sin and murmured against God that they did not have food. Their murmuring for food was similar to that of their murmuring at Marah for water.

When they felt shortage of food they remembered the food they had as slaves in Egypt and complained to Moses that this was a bad situation because even as slaves they had food in Egypt but now as free men they lacked food. They wished if they had the kind of food they had as slaves in the Egypt. They spoke as if they had no problems when they were slaves under

Pharaoh. They did not realize the importance of freedom God gave them and was leading them in their journey from Egypt to Canaan. Even though they were under the care of God they did not believe that God can take of their needs. It did not occur to them that God will provide them food just as he provided sweet water at Marah and rest at Elim.

The murmurings against Moses and Aaron were not accepted as justifiable by the LORD, yet the LORD had compassion on them. The LORD then told Moses that he will rain heavenly bread for them and people should go out and gather the food only to the extent that was need for them for the day.

Moses and Aaron said to the children of Israel that they will know how great the LORD was and is. The children of Israel aired their grievances against them saying that their murmurings are not against them but are against the LORD himself. Moses spoke to Aaron asking him to tell all the congregation of the children of Israel that the LORD, who brought them, heard their murmurings.

When the dew disappeared in the morning there appeared on the "face of the wilderness a small round thing as the hoar frost on the ground". The children of Israel saw the wonderful food and did not know what it was; and they called it as, "Manna".

When God rained food from heaven for the children of Israel, they wondered as to what it was. They asked one another, "what is it?" Moses said to them that it was the bread that was given to them by Jehovah. (Exodus 16:15). The children of Israel called the food as "Manna". The food was like coriander seed, white, and the taste of it was like wafers made with honey.

"And the house of Israel called the name thereof Manna: and it was like coriander seed, white; and the taste of it was like wafers made with honey" (Exodus 16:31)

Moses told them that they should gather only such quantity every day as is needed for the day and not store up for the next day; he continued saying that they are, however, allowed to gather two days food on the sixth day, so that they may rest on the seventh day.

And he said unto them, This is that which the LORD hath said, Tomorrow is the rest of the holy Sabbath unto the LORD: bake that which ye will bake to day, and seethe that ye will seethe; and that which remaineth over lay up for you to be kept until the morning. (Exodus 16:23)

There is a lesson for us to learn! It is not right on our part to murmur against the Lord; rather give thanks in all situations. Apostle Paul wrote in Philippians 4:19 for our exhortation and learning as follows: "But my God shall supply all your need according to his riches in glory by Christ Jesus".

Psalmist wrote:

"I have been young, and now am old; yet have I not seen the righteous forsaken, nor his seed begging bread.: (Psalms 37:25)

Why did God ask Moses that a Pot of Manna be kept in the Ark of the Covenant?

God specified a measure called "Omer" to the children of Israel and each individual was allowed to gather "manna' only that much a day. He, who gathered much more than that specified measure "Omer" had no more than what his actual need was for the day and he, who had gathered less had no lack of it.

There were some children of Israel in the camp who did not obey what Moses said to them. They gathered more food for the day than what was required. But, the excess food perished. The food they gathered on the sixth day for the seventh day, as instructed by God, did not perish, but lasted as fresh as it was gathered on the same day.

Moses was really antagonized at their behavior in gathering more than what was required for them. It was the heavenly bread, the "manna" that rained from heaven for them every day for six days in a week and not rained on the seventh day that they may take rest on that day signifying that it was His day.

Moses spoke to them and said that the LORD said that the seventh day was the rest day and it is holy Sabbath unto the LORD. He said to them that they should bake on the sixth day, soak in water that needs to be soaked in order that the excess food may last on the Sabbath day also. The food on the Sabbath day lasted as fresh as on the sixth day.

The food made on the previous day did not stink nor was any worm found in it on the Sabbath day. The LORD was not happy about their going out on the Sabbath day for food and he questioned Moses as to how long all of them refuse to obey His commandments and not take note of the provision of food He made for them on the sixth day that was sufficient for the seventh day also. Upon rebuke from Moses the people rested on the seventh day.

As the LORD commanded Moses, so did Aaron and laid a pot of 'Manna' up before the "Ark of the Covenant". And the children of Israel did eat manna forty years, until they came to a land inhabited; they did eat manna, until they came unto the borders of the land of Canaan" (Exodus 16:34-35)

In remembrance of God's provision of food to the children of Israel in the wilderness Moses told them that God commanded them to fill an "Omer" of it to be kept for future generations to see the bread that God gave them in the wilderness. He brought them out of the land of Egypt. Moses and Aaron took a pot and put in it -- an "omer" full of manna and deposited it before the Testimony. (an "Omer" is equivalent to tenth part of ephah, which is equivalent to seven and half pints, which is like five gallons – ref. Webster's Bible Dictionary). The children of Israel ate "manna" for forty years until they came to the borders of the land of Canaan.

THE TEN COMMANDMENTS

The children of Israel have departed from Rephidim and came to the wilderness of Sinai, where they camped on their journey to Canaan. At this time Moses went up unto God, who called him out of the mountain.

God instructed Moses to tell the children of Israel to recollect how He had delivered them from the bondage of slavery under Pharaoh. God also asked Moses to tell them to recollect how He bore them on eagle's wings and brought them unto Himself. God said to Moses to instruct the children of Israel that if they will obey His voice and keep His covenant, then they will be a peculiar treasure unto Him above all people.

Moses conveyed God's desire and instructions to the children of Israel and they unanimously answered together that they will obey God. Moses went to the LORD again and conveyed the words of the children of Israel that they all have answered and agreed to obey the voice of the Lord. (The details are mentioned in Exodus Chapter 19 and Chapter 20).

The Lord disciplined the children of Israel and gave to them the commandments and the law, which is known as the 'Mosaic Covenant'. God gave the Law and the covenant and this has become the governing factor for the children of Israel to lead their lives in holy manner pleasing to Him. It bound the children of Israel under certain laws and revealed their sin. The result was that they increased in their disobedience resulting in deaths. These laws were very stringent in nature and hard to follow.

The stringent requirements under law required religious life from the children of Israel. They were forced to look upon the Lord's commandments and ordinances and they tried to lead their lives following the commandments; yet they found that it was not possible to keep all the Ten Commandments and they committed sin. The law was taught to them by priests and the atonement of their sins was by sacrifices that the priests offered at the altar. No one could ever fulfill all the requirements of the law.

The 'Mosaic covenant' teach us that it is the ultimate sacrifice of Lord Jesus Christ upon the cross only that could save a sinner.

The Lord said to Moses that He will come in a thick cloud and speak to Moses in the presence of the children of Israel that they all may believe Moses as their leader for ever.

The LORD, as promised, came down on the third day after they have been sanctified on the first day and second day when they had washed their clothes. The Lord had set bounds for the children of Israel that they will not go up on to the Mount Sinai, and He said that only Moses could go up the mountain. If anyone had trespassed what the Lord said, one would die.

The Lord instructed that when the trumpet sounds long they all should go up to the mount but none will touch the borders of the mount Sinai, lest they die. Moses brought the children of Israel out of the camp to meet God and they all stood at the foot of the Mount Sinai.

At this time, as the Lord descended upon Mount Sinai the mount was altogether on a smoke and the smoke soared high as the smoke of a furnace and the mount shook greatly. The sound of the trumpet increased for them to hear it loudly. Moses spoke to God and God answered him by a voice.

There was great precaution taken by the children of Israel that they may not violate LORD's instructions; they knew that they would die if they violated the instructions. The strict instructions included that they should not gaze through to Jehovah. Moses assured Jehovah that the children of Israel cannot come up to Mount Sinai. Moses spoke to God and God answered him by a voice.

The Lord said Aaron and his sons and seventy priests could go up only to certain extent on the Mount Sinai to see from afar off God's manifestation of His glory, the glory of the God of Israel. Only Moses was allowed to go up the mountain Sinai to receive the two tablets on which God, with his finger, wrote the Ten Commandments in the presence of Moses. (Ex 19:24; 24:9-11)

The Ten Commandments are:

1. Thou shalt not have other gods before me.
2. Thou shalt not make any graven images.
3. Thou shalt not take the name of the Lord in vain
4. Remember to keep Sabbath holy
5. Honor thy father and mother
6. Thou shalt not murder
7. Thou shalt not commit adultery
8. Thou shalt not steal
9. Thou shalt not bear false witness
10. Thou shalt not covet thy neighbor's goods.

These Ten Commandments were very important ones given for the children of Israel to follow and observe them meticulously lest they face sever punishments that may include death.

Now, for New Testament believers Jesus gave two simple commandments. These two commandments contain the essence of The Ten Commandments and these two commandments are:

"And thou shalt love the Lord thy God with all thy heart, and with all thy soul, and with all thy mind, and with all thy strength: this is the first commandment.

And the second is like, namely this, Thou shalt love thy neighbour as thyself. There is none other commandment greater than these". (Mark 12:30-31)

Although it is not clearly said that the Ten Commandments should not be kept by New Testament believer the provision Lord Jesus Christ made for us to obey the two simple commandments shows the magnitude of love and grace he has towards us. These two commandments contain the meaning of all the Ten Commandments.

God knows that man can never keep the Ten Commandments, and therefore, he has extended grace for all those who confess to Him through

Jesus Christ, that any sin, except blasphemy of Holy Spirit will be forgiven by him.

We in this Grace period should realize that God shows us abundant mercy to anyone who confesses his sin to Him accepts Jesus Christ as the Lord and personal Savior.

"Moreover the law entered, that the offence might abound. But where sin abounded, grace did much more abound" (Romans 5:20)

As a remembrance of The LORD's promises, commandments, and the discipline that He has brought into the lives of the children and also for us to learn from their lives ways the LORD instructed that the two tablets on which the Ten Commandments were written should be kept in the 'Ark of the Testimony'.

CHAPTER 2
PRIESTS AND THEIR SERVICE

In Exodus Chapter 39 there is a description of how the children of Israel obeyed the instructions from the LORD through Moses about the construction of the Tabernacle and placement of various elements therein. They also obeyed the instructions of the choice of colors on the curtains and the garments for Aaron.

The cloths of service were made of the blue, the purple and the scarlet, and only these colors were to be used in the holy place. The ephod was made of gold, blue, purple, scarlet, and fine twined linen. In addition to many features that were on the garments of Aaron, a significant one that was noticeable was the breastplate that Aaron wore. It was foursquare set in four rows of precious stones.

The first row was of sardius, topaz, carbuncle,
The second row was of emerald, sapphire, and diamond,

The third row was of jacinth, agate, and amethyst, and

The fourth row was of a beryl, an onyx, and jasper.

These precious stones were according to the name of the twelve tribes of Israel. The binding of the breastplate by its rings unto the rings of the ephod with a lace of blue, skillfully woven, so that it may not fall away from the ephod. These instructions were meticulously carried out and Moses was pleased very much and he blessed the children of Israel.

The duties of priests are detailed in Exodus Chapters 28 and 29. The priest is required to be holy and set apart himself publicly for the service of God before ministering the people of God.

The priests chosen by God were Aaron and his children, and they were required to perform ceremonial solemnities to hollow themselves first, and then serve at the altar. They were required to bring unto the door of the tabernacle one young bullock, two rams without blemish, unleavened bread, made of wheat flour.

Speaking to Moses, God said that Aaron and his children should be anointed, consecrated, and sanctified in order that they may minister unto Him. Before they enter into the tabernacle, Aaron and his children were required to make sure that they were holy, and free from all iniquities. The warning was that if they fail in this regard and enter tabernacle with still iniquities in them, they would surely die.

Moses was asked to bring Aaron and his children before the tabernacle and wash them with water, put on Aaron the coat, the robe of ephod, the ephod, the breastplate and gird him with the girdle of the ephod.

In addition to these, Moses was also asked to put on Aaron's head the mitre, and the holy crown upon the mitre, and anoint him by pouring the oil over his head. Similarly, Moses was also asked to bring the sons of Aaron, and anoint them by putting bonnets on them. (Ephod is a linen apron, bonnet is a cap, breastplate is a metal piece worn around the body as a defensive armor, and mitre is a head-band used as a turban).

The stipulations God prescribed for priests were so stringent that they could not violate any of the conditions that God prescribed. These details are mentioned in Exodus Ch. 27, 28 and 29.

God gave Aaron and his sons the privilege to be the priests of perpetual statute. Later in Leviticus chapter 8 the description is given as to how Aaron and his sons would become consecrated priests unto God, after they have placed their hands upon the head of the bullock. The bullock was to be killed by Moses before the LORD, at the door of the tabernacle.

Moses would then have to take the blood of the

bullock and put it upon the horns of the altar with his finger and pour the entire blood at the bottom on one side of the altar. He also had to take the entire fat that covered the inwards, above the liver and the kidneys, and burn the fat upon the altar.

The flesh of the bullock and his skin and dung were to be burnt with fire outside the camp. This was sin offering. As instructed by God Moses took one ram, and Aaron and his sons placed their hands on the head of the ram.

Then, Moses killed the ram and took the blood of the ram and sprinkled it round about the altar. Moses, then cut the ram into pieces, and washed inwards and cut it into pieces and brought the entire pieces of the ram and burnt them upon the altar. This was burnt offering unto the LORD. Burnt offering was offered along with other sacrifices, namely, guilt offering, sin offering, new grain offering, sheaf offering, and free will offering.

God liked it so much so that this burnt offering is called as sweet savor made by fire unto the LORD. Moses then took the second ram, upon the head of which Aaron and his sons placed their hands. He killed the second ram and took the blood of the second ram, and applied it on the tip of the right ear, and upon the thumb and the right hands of Aaron and his sons.

In addition, he also applied the blood upon the great toe of their right foot, and sprinkled the blood upon the altar round about. He then, took the blood that was upon the altar and the anointing oil and sprinkled upon Aaron and upon his garments. Likewise, he did also the same upon the sons of Aaron. When such ceremonial solemnities were performed Aaron and his sons were hallowed.

The wave offering was done before the LORD when Moses placed in the hands of Aaron and in the hands of his sons, the fat and the rump, the fat that covered the inwards above the liver and the two kidneys, and the right shoulder of the ram, because the ram was the ram of consecration.

Along with these, one loaf of bread, and cake of oiled bread and one wafer out of the basket of the unleavened bread was also placed in the hands of Aaron and his sons. When such wave offering was offered before the LORD, Moses received from their hands the wave offering and burnt it upon the altar for a burnt offering and it was sweet savor before the LORD.

"And Moses took the breast, and waved it for a wave offering before the LORD: for of the ram of consecration it was Moses' part; as the LORD commanded Moses". (Leviticus 8:29)

These ceremonial solemnities extend to several

Chapters in Exodus and Leviticus. God desired that these should be observed meticulously.

"And the LORD came down upon Mount Sinai, on the top of the mount: and the LORD called Moses up to the top of the mount; and Moses went up" (Exodus 19:20)

The LORD himself descended onto Mount Sinai and He called Moses to the top of that mount and spoke to him. He gave 'Ten Commandments, and instructions as to how to worship Him in addition to explaining to him the details of the judgments and punishments for violating His commandments. These are described in Exodus Ch.19 to Ch.23.

The sacrifices offered in the Old Testament period were the shadows of the things that were to be fulfilled in Lord Jesus Christ. The sacrifices that were offered in the Old Testament period did not grant the true efficacy of redemption but were in essence similar to the deposit made for the perfect redemption in Lord Jesus Christ, who became perfect High Priest for us.

"And for this cause he is the mediator of the New Testament that by means of death, for the redemption of the transgressions that were under the first testament, they which are called might receive the promise of eternal inheritance". (Hebrews 9:15)

The book of Hebrews also shows us how Lord Jesus became our High Priest after the order of Melchizedek.

CHAPTER 3
ABRAM MEETS MELCHIZEDEK

Abram was called as "Hebrew" for the first in Genesis Chapter 14 which describes his triumph of the four kings who defeated confederacy of five kings and took Lot and his possessions along with other wealth they looted while dealing with the confederation of five kings.

The reason for this war was that the confederation of five kings rebelled against the four kings who earlier defeated these five kings and made them to serve them.

The four kings of east were: Amraphel, Arioch, Chedorlaomer, and Tidal(Genesis 14:1)
The five kings in Sodom and Gomorrah area were: Bera, Birsha, Shinab, Shemeber, and Bela (Genesis 14:2)

The five kings served the four kings for twelve years and in the thirteenth year they rebelled against those four kings. In the fourteenth year Chedorlaomer one of the four kings along others smote the five kings and took spoils of the land where Lot lived and Lot and others as prisoners. (Genesis 14:5-10)

It was at this time that a person came and told Abram, the Hebrew, about the looting of the wealth of the Sodom and Gomorrah and also of taking captive of his brother's son, Lot and his possessions.

Abram, who lived in Mamre peacefully and Lot, who lived in Sodom and Gomorrah, with his wealth, did not show interest in either party in these wars, but when Lot and his goods were looted Abram decided to wage war against the four kings to deliver his nephew, Lot and his possessions.

Abram had minority of army of trained three hundred and eighteen servants. He boldly went ahead and divided his army into different groups and smote the four kings and their army and pursued them unto Hobah, which is on the left hand of Damascus. He brought back his brother's son Lot and his wealth and also all the goods, and woman and the people.

Abram's victory against those kings was great and it was God who helped him to secure the said victory over the mighty armies of four kings. Several times in the scriptures it is be seen that numbers on the side of God do not matter when it comes to waging war with mighty men. Gideon's victory over Midianites, David's victory of Goliath and Philistines, and his victory at Ziklag over Amalakites, the fall of Jericho walls are only few examples to quote.

After the war was over there came two kings to

meet Abram after his victory. One was king of Sodom and other was king of Salem. King of Sodom offered Abram wealth and King of Salem offered bread and wine to Abram to have communion with him. Abram desired to have only the wealth that was stolen by the four kings and rejected rest of the wealth of this world and preferred to have fellowship with king of Salem.

The king of Salem was Melchizedek, about whom there is very little description. Melchisedek was king of righteousness and king of peace.

"And Melchizedek king of Salem brought forth bread and wine: and he [was] the priest of the most high God". Genesis 14:18

Surprisingly there appears one whom Scriptures call as "Melchizedek", king of Salem, and he was the priest of the most high God. This priest was even before the levitical priesthood came into existence. Abram paid tithe of all he got from his victory and Melchizedek blessed him.

There are two views about Melchizedek. One view is that he was Jesus Christ, who appeared to him. Few other times we see Christophany in the Old Testament; that is Lord Jesus Christ appearing in the form of man to help. One of the three men, who visited Abram was, believed to be Lord Jesus Christ (Genesis 18:1).

When Shadrach, Meshach, and Abednego were

thrown into fiery furnace King Nebuchadnezzar saw four persons in the fire. The fourth one was believed to be the Lord Jesus Christ protecting the three men. (Daniel 3:22-25).

Another view is that Melchizedek was a man, a type of Jesus Christ, in whom the anti-type Jesus fulfilled the priesthood. There is no mention about the lineage of Melchizedek in scriptures nor is any detailed description of him.

"And Melchizedek king of Salem brought forth bread and wine: and he was the priest of the most high God. And he blessed him, and said, Blessed be Abram of the most high God, possessor of heaven and earth: And blessed be the most high God, which hath delivered thine enemies into thy hand. And he gave him tithes of all". (Genesis 14:18-20)

What is interesting here is that Melchizedek brought "bread and wine" to Abram and that reminds us of Lord Jesus Christ who gave to his disciples bread and wine before his crucifixion and said to them "do this in remembrance of me".

"And as they were eating, Jesus took bread, and blessed [it], and brake [it], and gave [it] to the disciples, and said, Take, eat; this is my body. And he took the cup, and gave thanks, and gave [it] to them, saying, Drink ye all of it; For this is my blood of the new testament, which is shed for many for the remission of sins". Matthew 26:26-28

"And he took bread, and gave thanks, and brake [it], and gave unto them, saying, This is my body which is given for you: this do in remembrance of me". Luke 22:19

David prophesied about Jesus and wrote in Psalm 110:4 that Jehovah swore and will not repent of subduing the enemies of Lord Jesus Christ and bringing them to the footstool of Jesus, who was called as a priest for ever after the order of Melchizedek.

"The LORD hath sworn, and will not repent, Thou art a priest for ever after the order of Melchizedek". (Psalms 110:4)

Years later the writer of Hebrews wrote about Melchisedec in Hebrews Chapters 5,6 and 7.

So also Christ glorified not himself to be made an high priest; but he that said unto him, Thou art my Son, today have I begotten thee. As he saith also in another place, Thou art a priest for ever after the order of Melchisedec. (Hebrews 5:5-6)

"Whither the forerunner is for us entered, even Jesus, made an high priest for ever after the order of Melchisedec". (Hebrews 6:20)

Aaronic order of priesthood from Levites was

not perfect and Jesus became our high priest of the order of Melchisedec and this priesthood is for ever and ever. Lord Jesus Christ is our High Priest and the only mediator between God and men. All the believers in Christ are priests and have access to the most Holy God by Jesus (1 Peter 2:5).

"For he testifieth, Thou art a priest for ever after the order of Melchisedec" (Hebrews 7:17)

CHAPTER 4
THE SACRIFICES OFFERED
BY HIGH PRIEST

The LORD said unto Moses to speak to his brother and the LORD gave instructions, to Aaron through Moses, as detailed in the book of Leviticus Chapter 16. This is the sequence of sacrifices that were to be offered by Aaron, the high priest.

The sequence was followed by Jews ever since then until AD 70 when the Temple was destroyed. However, there is not much of evidence that they offer the sacrifices, after AD 70, just as the LORD gave commandment through Moses to Aaron.

During the reign of King Jeroboam, who ruled the Northern Province of Israel and King Rehoboam, who ruled over the Southern Province of Israel after King Solomon, the "House of Israel" was scattered. "The House of Israel" was taken captive by Assyrians, and the "House of Judah" was taken captive by Babylonians.

Later, some who were under the captivity under Babylonians returned to Southern Province of Israel and some preferred to stay in their regions where they were under captivity, perhaps because of the better life they enjoyed there.

Hebrew language was almost extinct and Israel was destroyed beyond recognition. But then, God promised that He will unite "The House of Israel" and "The House of Judah". Although Israel came back into existence on 14TH May, 1948, yet there is much to happen. There is no evidence that all the children of Israel have come into the land of Israel.

The Jews have very good knowledge about God and the commandments God gave to them through Moses and they are aware of all the ceremonial laws that were described in the Books of Moses.

Yet, it is surprising to note that they neither accept Jesus as their Messiah nor do they offer sacrifices, after AD 70, as detailed in the books of Moses, especially in the book of Leviticus.

Because Jesus was born as a Jew and God loved Israelites and called them as His People and the nation as His nation, and also because Bible asks us to pray for the peace of Jerusalem, I also pray for the peace of Jerusalem, I love them and I love Israel. I wish they all realized that Lord Jesus was divine and fully human when He was on this earth and died for the sake of our sins. He was buried, rose from the dead and ascended into heaven. He is seated on the right hand of the Majesty. He comes back again as soon as all His enemies are brought to His footstool. Scriptures say that if they do not believe Jesus as their Messiah now, they will be brought to their knees to acknowledge Jesus as their Messiah during the period of "Great Tribulation".

Their faith is that on the "Day of Atonement" they remember all their good works done and if the good works done during the past year outweigh their bad works they deem it as their forgiveness of their sins. If they do not sacrifice the offerings just they were asked to do in Leviticus Chapter 16 they owe explanation to the God's word which says:

"Come now, and let us reason together, saith the LORD: though your sins be as scarlet, they shall be as white as snow; though they be red like crimson, they shall be as wool". (Isaiah 1:18)

"But we are all as an unclean thing, and all our righteousnesses are as filthy rags; and we all do fade as a leaf; and our iniquities, like the wind, have taken us away". (Isaiah 64:6)

Here is how they were asked to offer sacrifices as detailed in Leviticus Chapter 16 on the "Day of Atonement".

On the "Day of Atonement" the high priest was to be all alone in the Tabernacle while the congregation waits outside the Tabernacle. There would be no priest to assist him in the sacrifices that he offers on that day. Any one assisting him on this day would be doing it outside the Tabernacle. The offerings are to be made by the high priest with high precision and reverence; otherwise his death was sure instantaneously.

The very fact that their present day high priests are not dying instantaneously for not offering the bullock and a ram for themselves and the Lord's goat as sin offering and confessing upon the live goat the sins of the high priest and the sins of the people followed by its letting loose into the wilderness itself shows that they are in violation of the Mosaic Law.

The high priest starts by washing his flesh in water and putting on linen garments. God commanded to lay aside the beautiful priestly garments of the high priest on this solemn occasion wherein the high priest is seen in a very humble stature, yet performing a very noble and pleasing deed for the Lord, while offering the sacrifices (Leviticus 16:4)

Lord Jesus Christ was stripped and was beaten up to a very humble state, yet performing a very noble and pleasing deed on the cross, while offering his own body and blood for the sake of remission of our sins. God loved us so much so that He gave His only begotten son for this purpose and whoever believes in Him shall not perish but have everlasting life. It is not we who loved Him first but He loved us first.

"And they stripped him, and put on him a scarlet robe". (Matthew 27:28)

The high priest was to take the bullock of the sin offering and make an atonement for him and for his house and kill it as sin offering on the altar (Leviticus 16:6)

Jesus was without any sin and without any blemish born of the Virgin Mary conceived of the Holy Ghost (Matthew 1:20) and, therefore, he did not need any bullock for himself, but He became the Lamb of God and the sacrifice for our sake. John testified of him that He was the Lamb of God who takes away the sin.

The high priest takes a censer full of burning coals of fire from off the altar before the LORD, and his hands full of sweet incense beaten small, and brings it within the veil. He puts the incense upon the fire before the LORD, so that the cloud of the incense may cover the mercy seat that is upon the ark of the testimony; and if he failed to follow the said method his death was sure.

The blood of the bullock is sprinkled with his finger upon the mercy seat eastward, and he sprinkles the blood before the mercy seat with his finger seven times. He goes back to the altar and kills the goat on which the lot fell as sin offering for the people and takes the blood of the goat within the veil and applies the blood and sprinkles just as he did with the blood of bullock for his own sake (Leviticus 16:15)

Jesus became the propitiation and substitution for our sake and fulfilled two-fold purpose of becoming sacrifice on behalf of us and bearing our sins upon himself as a substitute in our stead.

"Being justified freely by his grace through the redemption that is in Christ Jesus: Whom God hath set forth to be a propitiation through faith in his blood, to declare his righteousness for the remission of sins that are past, through the forbearance of God" (Romans 3:24-25)

Because the Tabernacle remained in the midst of the children of Israel with all their transgressions and uncleanness, Aaron, the high priest makes atonement for the holy place. He brings the live goat and lays both his hands upon the head of the live goat, signifying the transference of the sins of himself, and all the people of Israel on to the live goat, and confesses over the live goat all the iniquities of the children of Israel, and all the transgressions and all their sins, and sends it away by the hand of the fit man into the wilderness.

The goat carries the iniquities of all the people of Israel unto a land not inhabited never to return again to the land where the children of Israel lived. The live goat on which the sins are confessed is led outside the camp by a fit man into the wilderness (Leviticus 16:16-19).

He, who lets the goat into the wilderness bathes his flesh in water and afterwards comes into the camp. Notice the shedding of the blood and its sprinkling covered their sins, yet the sins remained in the sanctuary until the high priest transferred the sins onto the live goat which carried the sins far into an uninhabited land. The letting of the scapegoat into the wilderness is after the high priest changes his garments of linen and puts on his priestly garments and offering of the fat of the sin offering to be burnt upon the altar (Leviticus 16:20-22)

"For he hath made him to be sin for us, who knew no sin; that we might be made the righteousness of God in him". (2 Corinthians 5:21)

After the sin offering is made by the high priest he shall go into the tabernacle of the congregation and changes his clothing. The high priest washes his clothes, and bathes his flesh in water and then he goes into the camp in his priestly garments offers burnt offering. The high priest then offers burnt offering for himself first and then offers burnt offering for the people and makes atonement for himself and for the people. He burns the fat of the sin offering on the altar and then lets the scapegoat go.

He washes his clothes, bathes his flesh in water and afterward goes into the camp. The rest of the blood of the bullock and the Lord's goat which were killed for making atonement for sin offering will be carried outside the camp. The skins, their flesh, and their dung shall be burnt in the fire. He who burns the skins their flesh, dung washes his clothes and bathes his flesh in water and then shall come into the camp (Lev 16:27, 28).

The ritual is ordered by God as a statute to be observed on the tenth day of every seventh month in every year. God ordered that the children of Israel should mourn on this day. This is only one festival where the children of Israel are asked to mourn instead of rejoicing. It is the 'Day of Atonement", which is a national repentance day.

They and the strangers in that land and the sojourners in that land were not supposed to work on this day. The priest whom the high priest anoints on this day will serve as the High priest next in the stead of his father. He shall make atonement for the holy sanctuary, tabernacle, and the altar, and also priests, and for all the people of the congregation. This ritual was ordered to be a statute to be observed once every year and Aaron did as the LORD gave commandment through Moses.

"But Christ being come an high priest of good things to come, by a greater and more perfect tabernacle, not made with hands, that is to say, not of this building; Neither by the blood of goats and calves, but by his own blood he entered in once into the holy place, having obtained eternal redemption for us". (Hebrews 9:11-12)

For he testifieth, Thou art a priest for ever after the order of Melchisedec. (Hebrews 7:17)

We, in the New Testament period are so blessed that we are able to approach the Father, through our Lord Jesus Christ, who is our High Priest. We are all made royal priesthood.

CHAPTER 5
ROYAL PRIESTHOOD

"But ye are a chosen generation, a royal priesthood, an holy nation, a peculiar people; that ye should shew forth the praises of him who hath called you out of darkness into his marvellous light" (1 Peter 2:9)

1 Peter 2:9 lists the position of believers in the sight of our living God. Believers in Christ are a chosen generation, a royal priesthood, an holy nation, a peculiar people and then it lists the responsibilities of believer towards the One who has given such status before him. God called us from out of darkness into marvelous light in order that we may worship him, praise him and bear a good testimony for him.

The priests in the Old Testament period were required to offer sacrifices for themselves and then for the congregation which they were heading. It differed as the times changed and the way they offered sacrifices varied in different time periods.

Until the Mosaic Law came into existence individual saints in the Old Testament offered Sacrifices all by themselves that entitled them to be called as priests; and after the Law was proposed the entire congregations of the children of Israel were called the "Kingdom of

Priests", but because they violated the Law the priestly office was confined to the tribe of Levi. Aaron and his sons became the priests. The high priest could enter the Most Holy Place in the Tabernacle only once a year on the 'Day of Atonement'.

There are at least four individuals who can be taken for consideration. (1) Noah (2) Abraham (3) Isaac and (4) Jacob

Noah built an altar unto the Lord and offered clean beast, and clean fowl as burnt offerings on the altar. (Genesis 8:20) Abraham took two of his young men with him and Isaac his son and went to offer the burnt offering. (Genesis 22:3). Isaac built an altar and called upon the name of the Lord, and pitched his tent and his servants digged a well (Genesis 26:25). Jacob offered sacrifice upon the mount and called his brothers to eat bread and they ate the bread. (Genesis 31:54)

Then after the Law was proposed the children of Israel as a whole nation was called "kingdom of priests" (Exodus 19:6) But they violated the Law and antagonized God several times. They worshipped Idols and angered God. Then, God confined priesthood to the Tribe of Levi. Aaron and his sons from the Tribe of Levi were the priests. (Exodus 28:1)

"And hath made us kings and priests unto God

and his Father; to him be glory and dominion for ever and ever. Amen". (Revelation 1:6) This shows the priesthood of individual believers in the present age.

The sons of Aaron were anointed. They had on them Ephod, which is a linen apron, bonnet, which is a cap, breastplate, which is a metal piece worn around the body as a defensive armor, and mitre which is a head-band used as a turban. The stipulations God prescribed for priests were so stringent that they could not violate any of the conditions that God prescribed. These details are mentioned in Exodus Ch. 27, 28 and 29

Lord Jesus Christ was not after the order of Aaron but he was after the order of Melchizedek. While the priesthood of Aaron was limited; the priesthood of Melchizedek is for ever and ever. Even though there are not many references about Melchizedek, yet the references that are found in Genesis 14:18, Psalm 110:4, Hebrews 5:6 and in Hebrews Chapter 7 give us great knowledge about Lord Jesus Christ's Priesthood after the order of Melchizedek. Jesus is Priest, Prophet and King. Jesus became our High Priest because he offered himself as a sacrifice for our sins.

"For every high priest taken from among men is ordained for men in things pertaining to God, that he may offer both gifts and sacrifices for sins" (Hebrews 5:1)

"But into the second went the high priest alone once every year, not without blood, which he offered for himself, and for the errors of the people" (Hebrews 9:7)

"By a new and living way, which he hath consecrated for us, through the veil, that is to say, his flesh" (Hebrews 10:20)

Having therefore, brethren, boldness to enter into the holiest by the blood of Jesus, By a new and living way, which he hath consecrated for us, through the veil, that is to say, his flesh; And having an high priest over the house of God; Let us draw near with a true heart in full assurance of faith, having our hearts sprinkled from an evil conscience, and our bodies washed with pure water. (Hebrews 10:19-22)

According to Levite priesthood a priest could not be king and likewise a King could not be a priest. That is the reason why we see king Saul was not accepted by God as priest.

"And Saul said, Bring hither a burnt offering to me, and peace offerings. And he offered the burnt offering". (1 Samuel 13:9)

The result was seen in 1 Samuel 13:13

"And Samuel said to Saul, Thou hast done foolishly: thou hast not kept the commandment of the LORD thy God, which he commanded thee: for now would the LORD have established thy kingdom upon Israel for ever". (1 Samuel 13:13)

Melchizedek king of Salem was not of the order of Levites. Abraham gave him tithe to Melchizedek.

"And Melchizedek king of Salem brought forth bread and wine: and he was the priest of the most high God. And he blessed him, and said, Blessed be Abram of the most high God, possessor of heaven and earth: And blessed be the most high God, which hath delivered thine enemies into thy hand. And he gave him tithes of all". (Genesis 14:18-20)

"For this Melchisedec, king of Salem, priest of the most high God, who met Abraham returning from the slaughter of the kings, and blessed him" (Hebrews 7:1)

When Jesus was crucified the veil in the temple was rent into two from top to bottom signifying granting to us access to the Father through the Son of God, who is our High Priest. There is, therefore, no more a Priest required for us to offer sacrifices on our behalf nor are we required to confess our sins to any Priest in this world in order that he may convey to God our sins to be forgiven. We are all priests and he has given us the status of "Royal Priesthood" and Lord Jesus Christ is our High Priest and mediator. (Matthew

27:51)

"But Christ being come an high priest of good things to come, by a greater and more perfect tabernacle, not made with hands, that is to say, not of this building" (Hebrews 9:11)

We are given responsibility to offer sacrifices and those sacrifices are presenting our bodies as living sacrifice, holy and acceptable unto God. (Romans 12:1). We should be ready to help our brethren (1 John 3:16). We should visit the fatherless and widows in their affliction, and keep ourselves without any blemish. (James 1:27). We should offer sacrifices of praises and thanks to God continually. (Hebrews 13:15)

"I exhort therefore, that, first of all, supplications, prayers, intercessions, and giving of thanks, be made for all men". (1 Timothy 2:1)

CHAPTER 6
THE COLORS IN THE TABERNACLE

We will also see whether a New Testament believer should be legalistic to observe any color!

It is not without any significance that God instructed Moses to choose certain colors for the veils of the Tabernacle, and the robes of the priest. Pondering over the colors that God chose will reveal to us the importance of certain colors. God asked Moses to choose 'blue', 'purple' and 'scarlet' for the veils. The texture of the ten curtains that was to be used of the Tabernacle was made of 'fine twined linen', 'blue', 'purple, and 'scarlet'. (Exodus. 26:1)

In Genesis 49:12 there is a mention about Judah's teeth as white as milk. God says Judah is a lion's whelp and the scepter shall not depart from him. In Exodus 16:31 there is a mention about 'Manna', which was like coriander seed, white in color. White is an emblem of purity, innocence, strength and righteousness.

The color purple signifies the richness, affluence, pride, rare, and luxury. The robe of the high priest's was 'blue' in color. The rich man was clothed in purple and was in torment (Luke 16:23). The king in the book of Esther 8:15 had on him the garment of fine linen which was purple in color. The soldiers put on Jesus a purple robe (John 19:2).

Although Lazarus desired to be fed with the crumbs that fell from the table of the rich man, Lazarus left this earth to be in Abraham's bosom, while the rich man, who was clothed in purple, ended up in torments. The color 'scarlet' shines and is brilliant. In Isaiah 1:8 it is written that though our sins are like scarlet they shall be made as white as snow. In Song of Solomon there is a description of this color.

There it reads, "Thy lips are like a thread of scarlet..."

In Jeremiah 4:30 the color 'scarlet' (Crimson) is used in derision, like....

"And when thou art spoiled, what wilt thou do? Though thou clothest thyself with crimson... though thou rentest thy face with painting... thy lovers will despise thee, they will seek thy life".

In Revelation 17:4, Babylon the harlot was seen as arrayed in purple and scarlet with a golden cup in her hand full of abomination and filthiness of her fornication. When Moses had spoken every precept to the people of Israel, according to the law, he took the blood of calves, and of goats, with water, and scarlet wool, and hyssop, and sprinkled it upon both the book, and all the people. (Hebrews 9:19).

The colors in the curtains on the Tabernacle refer to certain important facts. The color, 'blue' refers to 'law', 'heaven', 'righteousness'. The color 'purple' refers to 'royalty', jealousy' and 'justice'. The color 'scarlet' also refers to 'sin' 'redemption' and 'suffering'. The undisputable fact is that we are redeemed from sin when Jesus, who was sinless, innocent, pure and holy, was made sin for us, and was mocked at, yet his blood cleansed us from sin and we are given the privilege to become the 'sons of God'.

What is it, then, for a New Testament believer? Should he be legalistic in following or prescribing certain colors for certain occasions or for ceremonies? Well, if we like a particular color, we may go ahead with choosing that color; but let it not be done on compulsion or as legalistic necessity.

Apostle Paul's answer to the question of observing days, months, times and years or to judge in meat, or in drink or in respect of holyday is as follows:

But now, after that ye have known God, or rather are known of God, how turn ye again to the weak and beggarly elements, whereunto ye desire again to be in bondage? Ye observe days, and months, and times, and years. I am afraid of you, lest I have bestowed upon you labour in vain.

(Galatians 4:9-11)

Let no man therefore judge you in meat, or in drink, or in respect of an holyday, or of the new moon, or of the sabbath days: (Colossians 2:16)

So, then, let us not have a legalistic view about colors as well. Having a legalistic view about observing colors is similar to that of having legalistic view about observing days.

CHAPTER 7
THE MYSTERY REVEALED

The significance of the four rows of precious metals with the names of the twelve tribes of Israel written and placed on the breastplate of Aaron the priest, who enters the Holy place to offer incense at the Golden Altar, shows us the love of God toward the children of Israel. These are the children of Israel, whom God never forgets and offered them the salvation.

The Son of God, Jesus Christ came into the world to save the children of Israel, who were lost, but they rejected Him as Messiah. That paved the way for the Gentiles to enter into the Holy place of God.

Apostle Paul writes about this mystery in Romans 11:25 about which we should not be ignorant of and that the blindness in part happened to Israel, so that the fullness of the Gentiles should come in. Apostle Paul goes on in Romans 16:25 that God will establish us according to the gospel and the preaching of Jesus Christ that this mystery, which was kept secret since the world began, is revealed in the New Testament period. Paul confirms it in Ephesians 1:9 that God made known to us the mystery of His will in accordance with His good pleasure that He had purposed in Himself. God

hid this mystery about granting salvation to
Gentiles from the beginning of the world, even
that mystery that was hid from ages and from
generations but now is revealed to His saints.
When we ponder on these few verses, namely,
Ephesians 3:9, Colossians 1:26, 27 the love of
God for every one whether it be Jew or Gentile is
clearly known.

God chose the children of Israel and His own, and
called Jacob as His first born. No one can call
himself, as Israel, except Jacob and his twelve
children. Those who are not the children of Jacob
and yet call themselves as Jews are rendering
themselves to be called as 'synagogue of Satan'.

"I know thy works, and tribulation, and poverty,
(but thou art rich) and I know the blasphemy of
them which say they are Jews, and are not, but
are the synagogue of Satan". (Revelation 2:9)

God promised them to bring them out of the
affliction of Egypt and on their way they had
defeated six nations. He gave them the 'law' to
follow meticulously and protected them. Yet they
committed sins again and again on their journey
to the promised land of Canaan, which God said
is a land flowing with milk and honey.

When Jesus began to teach by the sea side when
multitudes gathered He spoke to them in
parables, but when His twelve disciples asked
Him why He spoke in parables, He said to them:

"And he said unto them, Unto you it is given to know the mystery of the kingdom of God: but unto them that are without, all these things are done in parables" (Mark 4:11)

The woman of Canaan, who came to Jesus crying to Him, calling Him, "O Lord, thou Son of David" and prayed to Him to heal her daughter, who was vexed with a devil, Jesus first did not answer her. When the disciples of Jesus asked Him to send her away, He said, that He was sent unto the lost sheep of the house of Israel and it was not right for Him to take the bread from the children and cast it to dogs.

When Jesus heard that she humbled herself and worshipped Him ceaselessly with faith he granted her prayer. She said to Him that even the dogs ate the crumbs that fell from the master's table. When Jesus had compassion on her and granted her desire, her daughter was made whole that very hour.

CHAPTER 8
THE INTERCESSION
OF MOSES

It was consoling and so comforting to Israel that
Moses chose to intercede on their behalf,
because just a little while ago Moses was very
much displeased with them when they made an
idol and worshipped it. When Moses returned
from the mount Sinai with two tablets written on
them with the finger of God, the Ten
Commandments, he saw Aaron and the children
of Israel had made a calf of gold and were
worshipping it. They even went to the extent of
stripping themselves and worshiping the idol in
their nakedness (Exodus 32:25)

Moses was very angry to look at that situation
and ordered that whoever was on the Lord's side
may gather on his side. The sons of Levi joined
him. Moses ordered a great slaughter of their
brothers and companions. The children of Levi
obeyed him and there fell three thousand men.
Then Moses asked them to consecrate
themselves to the LORD that He may bless them.
On the next morning, Moses said to them that
they sinned greatly and, therefore, he decided to
return to the LORD to make atonement for their
sins.

Just as he said, Moses returned to the LORD and

said to HIM that the children of Israel sinned greatly, but they should be forgiven of their sins. Moses, being their leader, offered that the LORD may blot out his name from the book of life if the LORD was so angry at them that He cannot forgive their sins. Every intercession of Moses was so powerful mediation that the LORD had mercy on Israel time and again and showed his love for the children of Israel.

The LORD was pleased with Moses and He said to Moses that He will blot out whoever sinned, in due course of time when He visits them, but for now he may return to them and lead them. The LORD plagued the people, because they made the calf, which Aaron made as an idol, for them.

The LORD gave instructions to Moses to move on so that He could fulfill the promise He made and swore unto the Abraham, Isaac, and Jacob, that He will deliver the children of Israel from all their enemies. The LORD promised to Moses that He will send an angel before him, and will drive out all the gentile nations -- the Canaanites, the Amorites, the Hittites, the Perizzites, the Hivites and the Jubusites. The LORD called the children of Israel as "stiff necked people" (Exodus 33:3).

CHAPTER 9
THE INTERCESSORY PRAYER
OF LORD JESUS CHRIST

Lord Jesus Christ's intercessory prayer was greater than that of Moses. Lord Jesus Christ lifted up His eyes as He prayed in Gethsemane, and invoked the love of the Father in heaven, and sought help from Him to be always with His disciples. Just before He was crucified He prayed to the Father in Heaven that He had finished the work that He had embarked upon to finish in this world.

Jesus glorified Him and prayed that just as He had glorified the Father in heaven, He may be glorified with the glory that He had with Him even before the world was. Jesus prayed for his disciples and then for everyone. It is that prayer that brought us under the tender care of the Father in heaven. Jesus prayed that not only His disciples need to be protected but all those, who believed on the word through them, need to be protected.

"Neither pray I for these alone, but for them also which shall believe on me through their word". (John 17:20)

Therefore, it becomes mandatory on the part of believers in Christ to have intercessory prayers and invoke help, guidance, and protection from our God through His Son Jesus Christ.

The prayer of Jesus, as we read in John Chapter 17, before he was betrayed for crucifixion has some significant truths. There are three divisions clearly seen in the prayer of Jesus. Firstly, he prayed for himself, secondly he prayed for his disciples, thirdly he prayed not for the world but for those who believe on him through the message of his disciples.

John Chapter 17:1-5 contain Jesus' prayer for himself, John 17:6-10 contain Jesus' prayer for his disciples and John 17:11-26 contain Jesus' prayer for those who believe on Jesus through the message of his disciples.

In the prayer for himself he glorified the Father and said that he has glorified the Father and that he may be glorified likewise. Jesus lifted up his eyes to heaven and said to the Father that hour is come and prayed that the Son may glorify the Father.

Jesus says that the Father gave power to the Son over all flesh that the Son may give eternal life to as many as the Father gave to the Son. Jesus prays that those who believe in him may have the life eternal that they might know the Father, who is the only true God, and Jesus Christ whom the Father sent. Jesus had earlier said the Father and the Son are one. "I and my Father are one"

(John 10:30) and John 14:6 reads "Jesus saith unto him, I am the way, the truth, and the life: no man cometh unto the Father, but by me". (John 14:6)

Jesus prayed to the Father that he may be glorified in the Father with the glory that the Son had with the Father before the world was. (Cf. John 17:1-5) He continued his prayer and says that he glorified the Father and finished the work that the Father assigned to him.

Later, his disciple Peter explained about the glory that the Son of God, Lord Jesus Christ relinquished and came down to this earth in the form of servant and made in the likeness of men. Lord Jesus Christ was in the form of God, and yet he did not think it robbery to be equal to be with God and made himself of no reputation.

"He humbled himself and became obedient unto death, even the death of the cross". Jesus came down to this earth to save sinners. The Father exalted him and gave him the name above every name "that at the name of Jesus every knee should bow, of the things in heaven, and things in earth, and things under the earth".

Every tongue will confess him that Jesus Christ is the Lord to the glory of the Father. (Cf. Philippians 2:6-11)

At the trial before Pilate Jesus was asked

questions. Pilate asked him if Jesus was the King of the Jews. In answer Jesus asked Pilate if he was asking this question on his own or did someone ask him to inquire about Jesus.

Pilate vehemently asserted that he was not Jew and that the nation of Jesus and the chief priests delivered him to Pilate.

Jesus said that his kingdom is not of this world, but his kingdom is yet to come. Pilate continues his questions and asked Jesus if Jesus was the king of the Jews. Jesus said that Pilate had said so and for this reason he was born and for this reason he came into the world that he should bear witness unto the truth. Jesus said that everyone who is of the truth will hear his voice. When people desired that Barabbas be released in preference to Jesus Pilate released Barabbas and scourged Jesus (Cf. John 18:33-40)

"Then Pilate therefore took Jesus, and scourged him". (John 19:1)

Pilate questioned Jesus as to where Jesus was from and Jesus did not give him any answer. Pilate then boasted saying the he had the power to crucify Jesus or to realize him. But then, Jesus said to Pilate that he had no power over Jesus except it was given to him from above. (John 19:9-11) The people cried there that Jesus be crucified

"Then answered all the people, and said, His blood be on us, and on our children". (Matthew 27:25)

Pilate then, delivered Jesus to be crucified.

"Then delivered he him therefore unto them to be crucified. And they took Jesus, and led him away". (John 19:16)

CHAPTER 10
HE IS RISEN

"And when the sabbath was past, Mary Magdalene, and Mary the mother of James, and Salome, had bought sweet spices, that they might come and anoint him. And very early in the morning the first day of the week, they came unto the sepulcher at the rising of the sun. And they said among themselves, Who shall roll us away the stone from the door of the sepulcher? And when they looked, they saw that the stone was rolled away: for it was very great". (Mark 16:1-4)

On the day when Jesus was tried before Pontius Pilate the governor, there was option for people to have either Jesus released or Barabbas released. It was feast day and according to their custom a prisoner of their choice could be released. Pilate asked the people as to who they prefer to be released; whether it was Barabbas or Jesus.

The people cried that Barabbas, a notable criminal be released in preference to that of innocent Jesus. (Matthew 27:15-18) Pilate knew that Jesus was innocent and that is why he asked the people as to what evil Jesus had committed. A great politician as he was, Pontius Pilate did not want to offend Herod on one side and the people on the other. But the people cried more that Jesus should be crucified. "And the governor said, why, what evil has he done? But they cried out the more, saying, Let him be crucified. (Matthew 27:23) Then Pilate washed his hands and justified himself saying: "I am innocent of the blood of this just person: see you to it". (Matthew 27:24) Pilate acknowledged that Jesus was just person, yet he has handed over Jesus to the choice of people. Thus Pilate is guilty of not showing the justice.

After the Sabbath was past early in the morning Mary Magdalene, and Mary the mother of James went to the tomb where Jesus was laid. A rich man of Arimathaea, named Joseph, who also himself was Jesus' disciple begged for the body of Jesus and he laid it in his own new tomb.
.
And laid it in his own new tomb, which he had hewn out in the rock: and he rolled a great stone to the door of the sepulchre, and departed. (Matthew 27:60)

On the tomb, where the dead body of Jesus was laid, a great stone was rolled over it. The tomb was closed with that great stone and it was sealed so that no one could remove the body of Jesus or steal the body of Jesus. All the accusers took care that the dead body of Jesus was not removed from the tomb. The tomb was guarded so that no one could remove or steal the body of Jesus.

"Pilate said unto them, You have guards: go your way, make it as sure as you can. So they went, and made the sepulcher sure, sealing the stone, and setting a guard". (Matthew 27:65-66)

But then, as per the prophecy and as Jesus told beforehand, he rose from the dead and went to Galilee before Mary Magdalene and Mary the mother of James reached the tomb.

Jesus had told that he will rise on the third day, and yet these two missed the timing very badly. Not only this, but before they reached the tomb, they had a big question in their minds as to who will role away the stone?

However they found answer to their question when the Angel of the Lord announced that he rose from the dead.

And, behold, there was a great earthquake: for the angel of the Lord descended from heaven, and came and rolled back the stone from the door, and sat upon it. (Matthew 28:2)

And the angel answered and said unto the women, Fear not: for I know that you seek Jesus, who was crucified. He is not here: for he is risen, as he said. Come, see the place where the Lord lay. (Matthew 28:5-6)

Lord Jesus Christ is coming again soon! But then,

why do we feel He is delaying to come?

"The Lord is not slack concerning his promise, as some men count slackness; but is longsuffering to us-ward, not willing that any should perish, but that all should come to repentance". (2 Peter 3:9)

CHAPTER 11
UNTIL HIS ENEMIES ARE BROUGHT TO HIS FOOTSTOOL

Psalm 110:1-7 "The LORD said unto my Lord, Sit thou at my right hand, until I make thine enemies thy footstool. The LORD shall send the rod of thy strength out of Zion: rule thou in the midst of thine enemies. Thy people shall be willing in the day of thy power, in the beauties of holiness from the womb of the morning: thou hast the dew of thy youth. The LORD hath sworn, and will not repent; Thou art a priest for ever after the order of Melchizedek.

The Lord at thy right hand shall strike through kings in the day of his wrath. He shall judge among the heathen, he shall fill the places with the dead bodies; he shall wound the heads over many countries. He shall drink of the brook in the way: therefore shall he lift up the head"

This psalm is fully a gospel concerning our Lord Jesus Christ, who executes the office of a prophet, of a priest, and of a king. The Father in heaven promises a prophetical office to Lord Jesus in verse 2, a priestly office in verse 4, and kingly office in verses 1, 3, and 5 to 6. The Jews never accepted this fact lest they should accept Jesus as their Messiah. Stephen gazing into heaven testifies in Acts 7:55 that he "saw the glory of God, and Jesus standing on the right hand of God". Paul an Apostle of Lord Jesus Christ writes in Ephesians 1:20 that "... he wrought in Christ, when he raised him from the dead, and set him at his own right hand in the heavenly places".

The writer of Hebrews writes in Hebrews 1:3 that Lord Jesus "...being the brightness of his glory, and the express image of his person, and upholding all things by the word of his power, when he had by himself purged our sins, sat down on the right hand of the Majesty on high". He is our high priest, "We have such an high priest, who is set on the right hand of the throne of the Majesty in the heavens" (Hebrews 8:1) and "...after he had offered one sacrifice for sins for ever, sat down on the right hand of God" (Hebrews 10:12).

Recalling the Psalm of David, where David called Lord Jesus as his Lord and the Son of God, Jesus points this fact to Pharisees, who often tried to trap him. Pharisees of old believed that David said these verses about the Messiah, and yet the modern Pharisees denied this fact. When Jesus pointed this fact in Mark 12:36

"For David himself said by the Holy Ghost, The LORD said to my Lord, Sit thou on my right hand, till I make thine enemies thy footstool", they were speechless. Jesus then said in Mark 12:38-40 "...Beware of the scribes, which love to go in long clothing, and love salutations in the marketplaces, And the chief seats in the synagogues, and the uppermost rooms at feasts: Which devour widows' houses, and for a pretence make long prayers: these shall receive greater damnation".

Immediately after the prophesy about the LORD making all the enemies of Lord Jesus Christ to come to his footstool is complete the second coming of Lord Jesus will take place and the Church will have rapture into the clouds to meet him in the air.

The time and seasons are known only to the Father in heaven. Matthew 24:36 "But of that day and hour knoweth no man, no, not the angels of heaven, but my Father only".

The advent of the Lord Jesus on this earth will be after the false teachers have brought in heresies and wrong doctrines among Christians and false prophets saying that Jesus has already come and he is 'here' and/or 'there' and after the revealing of the 'man of sin', the 'son of perdition', who is Antichrist. Jesus warned us to be careful not to believe when false prophets say,"Lo, here is Christ, or there..." Matthew 24:23

It is time to realize that one should not harden his heart but yield to the will of God and accept Lord Jesus Christ as personal Savior. It is time to confess that Lord Jesus died on behalf of us on the cross, was buried and rose from the dead. If we believe in Him He will forgive us our sins. It is by grace through faith in Him that one will be saved and will have everlasting life in Him.

CHAPTER 12
YIELD TO THE WILL OF GOD

" For that ye [ought] to say, If the Lord will, we shall live, and do this, or that" James 4:15

James, an Apostle of Jesus Christ warns that a believer should never say that he will do something on his own. It is wrong on the part of believer to say that "today or tomorrow we will go into such a city, and continue there a year, and buy and sell, and get gain".

This sort of statement-making by believer shows that the believer can live by himself, without the help of God. The statement shows that he is capable of achieving something on his own. It is an assertion by the believer that he can go with his friend either today or tomorrow to a place of gain, continues to live there for a year, buy, sell, and make profit. He makes statement as if God's help is not required and he can do all by himself, even buy, sell and make profit.

The Word of God says that man does not know what the next day may bring forth in man's life. The man, who makes such statement, does not know that his life is like a vapor, which appears but for a little while, and then vanishes. No one on this earth can exactly say what the next moment can bring forth in his/her life.

Therefore, the Word of God, exhorts us that we should always say "if God is willing", before making a firm statement. Man can never be sure of his future. Believer should learn to say "if God is willing that I live"; He should prefix "If God is willing" before making any firm statement and continue to say, I would do this or that.

Humble nature of a believer only can make his heart to yield to the will of God. Pride and grace are just opposite to one another. If we are proud of our achievements, and capabilities, we will fail, but if we depend on the grace of God he draws near to us, and helps us in times of our trouble. Submit, therefore, always to the Will of God, and resist the devil.

"Submit yourselves therefore to God. Resist the devil, and he will flee from you. " James 4:7

KISS THE SON
"Kiss the Son, lest he be angry, and ye perish from the way, when his wrath is kindled but a little. Blessed are all they that put their trust in him". (Psalms 2:12)

Psalmist having said in Psalms chapter 1 that the godly should not have company with ungodly now wonders as to why the ungodly and sinners imagine vain things such as to ridicule the living God and work against the children of the living God.

Those who are saved in the precious blood of Jesus Christ are the Children of God. Apostle Paul writes: "For ye are all the children of God by faith in Christ Jesus" (Galatians 3:26).

Mighty kings, princes, wise men, and dictators have come and gone but none lived and ruled like our living God who is eternal. He rules the earth; he is there everywhere. Man's thoughts are not God's thoughts. His ways are higher than ours. He is mightier than anybody. When man takes refuge in his own strength and wisdom the Lord will have him in derision.

The Father says He has set Jesus upon the holy hill of Zion. This is a prophecy and it is about the thousand year peaceful reign of our Lord Jesus Christ from the throne of David. The Father promises that the uttermost parts will be given to The Son for his possession. Jesus is the Son of God and he shall break the mighty men with iron rod and he breaks them as the rod strikes a potter's vessel.

There were mighty men such as Sihon, king of Amoties, Og, the king of Bashaan, and Goliath in Philistine army but none prevailed against God and the children of Israel.

Sihon, king of the Amorites, opposed and tried to prevent in vain the Israelites to pass through his territory. The result was that he was defeated and Israelites not only took possession of his cities but they had their way through the land of Amorites. (Numbers 21:21-24)

Og, the king of Bashan, who was ruler over sixty cities went out against Israelites but God assured Moses of his help and he defeated Og, the king of Bashan and took possession of his land. (Numbers 21:33-35)

There was a mighty man in Philistine army and he was Goliath. But David, a shepherd boy, son of Jessy, with the help of the Almighty God defeated Goliath miraculously when he slang one smooth stone from his sling that struck on his forehead and Goliath fell face down on the ground. David pulled out Goliath's sword from his sheath and killed him.

There were other mighty men like Alexander the great, Napoleon, Hitler, etc. Some of them were great and some of them were terror to others; but all of them died.

Many dictators who stood strong defiantly in the recent past fell down and lost their positions. Above all one that rules is our living God and His only begotten Son, Lord Jesus Christ is our Savior. Are we greater than these mighty men? If not, then let us depend upon the living God and worship him.

Psalmist points to antitype in Psalm Chapter 2 and exhorts, therefore, to serve Jesus with fear and rejoice. There is an interesting phrase used and it is "Kiss the Son". It is not an advice for us to kiss our sons but it is an exhortation to worship the Son of God, Lord Jesus Christ. It is very good that we kiss our sons, but here in this context it is not an exhortation to kiss our sons but it is an exhortation to worship the Son of God, Lord Jesus Christ.

There is warning that if we do not worship the Son of God he would be angry and we may perish from the way. Psalmist says that those who put their trust in the Lord will be blessed.

Let us say as the children of Israel said when Joshua challenged them with a question as to whom they prefer to serve; whether it is idols or the living God! They all answered and said without any hesitation: "We will serve the LORD".

"And the people said unto Joshua, Nay; but we will serve the LORD". (Joshua 24:21)

It is time that we realize that we should keep away from evil counsel and listen to the word of God and respond to His call. He is faithful and just to forgive us our sins.

CHAPTER 13
KEEP ME FROM THE
COUNSEL OF THE WICKED

"Hide me from the secret counsel of the wicked; from the insurrection of the workers of iniquity" Psalm 64:2

Apostle Paul was still a prisoner as we read in Acts Chapter 27 and he was to be brought before Caesar. God's purposes will never fail no matter what man plans to do or what hurdles one might encounter.

The charge of taking Paul and other prisoners was given to a Centurion named Julius. Paul was arrested on false charges and ever since he was arrested he was defending that he was preaching the word of the living God. God not only delivered Paul from the shipwreck but others accompanying Paul also escaped death. The ship in which they were sailing had a wreck and broke into pieces but none in the ship lost life.

"And we were in the ship, all the souls, two hundred and seventy-six". (Acts 27:37) Every one of the two hundred seventy six people who were onboard the ship was saved. It was in the plan of God that Paul be brought before Caesar and it was done according to the purposes of

God. Julius, the Centurion was kind to Paul, yet he refused to pay heed to the wise words of Paul not to venture out on sailing from 'Fair Havens' where they were resting for a while. The wind was contrary, but when the Centurion and others saw that south wind blew softly they gave credence to the master and the owner of the ship.

Paul had forewarned them that the voyage will be with much loss and damage, yet the Centurion and others took counsel among themselves and the master of the ship for granted. Not much time had elapsed when they all encountered a violent tempest which resulted in the ship getting uncontrollable. They sailed further and their final arrival at a place got their ship stuck in the creek. The front portion of the ship got firmly stuck in the creek and the rear portion broke into pieces.

The shipmen and others tried to escape from the boat, but Paul advised them contrary that they all should stay in the ship if they want their lives to be saved.

The soldiers tried to kill those who were onboard the ship but Paul stood firm that they should not kill any one. Finally Centurion heard the words of Paul and commanded that those who knew swimming should cast themselves first into the sea and swim out to the land, and the rest should swim out to the land holding fast the broken pieces of the ship.

Notice that God's plan through his servant prevailed and the counsel of the human beings failed. They had rescue boats to escape but could not be used. They planned to kill the sailors but failed. They saw south wind blew softly and were impatient and put their plans at work and suffered loss and damage. They refused the counsel of the spirit-filled God's servant and took the counsel of the worldly and reaped bad consequences.

"I have fought a good fight, I have finished my course, I have kept the faith" 2 Timothy 4:7

CHAPTER 14
PROVISION OF SALVATION

Over and over the children of Israel murmured against the LORD while they were on their journey from Egypt to Canaan. God knew of their failures and warned them several times. He even chastised them in order that they may come back to him.

Although God did miracles and delivered them from the bondage of slavery under Pharaoh, and led them through wilderness by providing them heavenly 'manna' as their food, and protecting them during day by pillar of cloud and during night by pillar of fire to give them to lead them the way and give them (Exodus 13:21), yet they angered him by rebelling against him. They did not hearken unto God; "...they did not every man cast away the abominations of their eyes, neither did they forsake the idols of Egypt: then I said, I will pour out my fury upon them, to accomplish my anger against them in the midst of the land of Egypt" (Ezekiel 20:8)

The children of Israel spoke against God and against Moses. Therefore, God sent fiery serpents among them and they bit them and many people of Israel died. But when the people of Israel, who were still alive, came to Moses and said to him that they have sinned against God and requested

Moses to pray on behalf of them, he prayed to the Lord.

The LORD answered Moses' prayer. As per the commandment of God Moses made a serpent of brass and put it upon a pole. Whoever of those bitten by serpents looked at the serpent of brass lived. (Numbers 21:8-10).

Oh! What a great provision God made for the children of Israel to be saved. It is not only by looking unto the brazen serpent that they lived but by doing so, they obeyed God's commandment and it was counted unto them that they looked at God for their salvation. And, God honored their faith and gave them life.

John the Baptist recollects this provision when he spoke about it in John 3:14-15. He was pointing to the Son of God, whom he identified as "the lamb of God" who is our Lord Jesus Christ, born of the Virgin Mary, and he was also called the Son of Man. He dwelt among us in flesh. John, the Baptist said that He must be lifted up just as the brazen serpent was lifted up in the wilderness in order that "whosoever believeth on him should not perish, but have eternal life" Jesus was lifted up on the cross and he died for us bearing our sin.

We should, therefore, be looking unto Jesus who is the author and finisher of our faith. He endured the cross with joy despising shame. He

died for our sake, rose from the dead on the third
day, ascended into heaven and seated on the
right hand of the Father. Bible says that if a man
is not born-again, he will not see the Kingdom of
God. For everyone, who did not yet receive
salvation, it is necessary, therefore, that one
must receive Jesus as personal savior by faith in
him. (Hebrews 1:3 and 12:2)

The Lord says: "Come unto me, all ye that labour
and are heavy laden, and I will give you rest"
(Matthew 11:28)
The Greatness of God

"He shall feed his flock like a shepherd: he shall
gather the lambs with his arm, and carry them in
his bosom, and shall gently lead those that are
with young". (Isaiah 40:11)

Isaiah prophesied about Lord Jesus Christ seven
hundred years ago that he is almighty One, and
the government shall be upon him. Indeed, he is
the Son of God, the very image of invisible God,
who came and dwelt among us in flesh. Who has
understood him fully? God is Triune, the Father,
the Son, and the Holy Spirit. Jesus said that he
and the Father are one and whoever has seen
him has seen the Father.

Isaiah speaks of the Good shepherd, who keeps
his flock. In Isaiah 40:11 he says Good shepherd
feeds his flock and shall gather the lambs with
his arm. He carries them in his bosom and gently

leads those that are young. He walks with them slowly at their pace. He guards the sheep waiting at the doorway because he is the keeper and he is the door. No one can come to the Father but by him. No thief can enter to steal the lamb unless he steps on the watching shepherd. No wolf can enter unless it encounters the shepherd first. The shepherd has the courage, power and strength to lay his life for the sake of his sheep.

A man may think what a shepherd can do with that little staff in his hand! Do we remember the staff in the hands of Moses that God used to humble the proud Pharaoh?

Yes, Indeed the Lord God is so mighty and powerful that created the heavens and the earth. He is the One who measured the waters in the hollow of his hands. He is the One, who laid sand as the boundaries for oceans. He is the One, who can measure the stretch of the heaven with the span of his hand. Heaven is his throne and the earth is his footstool. He sits on the circle of the earth and rules the inhabitants thereof. He is the One, who does not take counsel from anybody.

Who could instruct him? Who could show him the path of judgment? He is the righteous judge. He cares for the poor in Spirit; he blesses those, who are humble in heart. He is the God of comfort. He is our Lord, He is our Savior. He is eternal and he wants us to be with him eternally.

Do you have a question as to how God, who is Omnipresent and so big can measure the heavens? Indeed, it is tough to understand. If we can understand how God, who is so big, could take the form of man and be born to Virgin Mary, then it would not be hard to understand how God could measure the heavens.

"Who hath measured the waters in the hollow of his hand, and meted out heaven with the span, and comprehended the dust of the earth in a measure, and weighed the mountains in scales, and the hills in a balance? Who hath directed the Spirit of the LORD, or being his counsellor hath taught him? With whom took he counsel, and who instructed him, and taught him in the path of judgment, and taught him knowledge, and shewed to him the way of understanding?" (Isaiah 40:12-14)

CHAPTER 15
SALVATION FOR EVERY ONE

"Ho, everyone that thirsteth, come ye to the waters, and he that hath no money; come ye, buy, and eat; yea, come, buy wine and milk without money and without price". (Isaiah 55:1)

Isaiah Chapter 53 had prophecy about the crucifixion of Jesus Christ and Isaiah Chapter 54 has blessings and protection to the Children of Israel. In Isaiah Chapter 55 there is a call for every one which includes you and me. The calling is for everyone who thirsts to come to the waters. This is a call for salvation which is available free of cost but there should be thirst to have it.

he salvation is to be sought for. There needs to be desire to have it and there needs to be desire to accept it free of cost. God does not want any of our works or money to be used for receiving that which is given free of cost and the price for which is already paid for. The price is paid for by Jesus Christ on the cross.

Matthew Chapter 13:44-46 describe the desire one has to have to receive the kingdom of heaven, which is like a treasure hidden in a field. The parable says that when a man finds the field that has treasure in it, he goes and sells his entire assets and buys that field. Also it is compared to an expensive pearl that a man buys by selling his entire assets. Luke Chapter 14:33 says that, whoever does not forsake all that he has, cannot become the disciple of Jesus Christ. Salvation is so precious but it cannot be bought with silver and gold.

The Lord says that his thoughts are higher than ours and his ways are higher than ours. His thoughts are not our thoughts and his ways are not our ways. "For my thoughts are not your thoughts, neither are your ways my ways, saith the LORD" (Isaiah 55:8)

The wise man says in Proverbs that there is a way that seems good for a man but it leads to destruction. "There is a way which seemeth right unto a man, but the end thereof are the ways of death". (Proverbs 14:12) When God interferes in the lives of believers it is for chastening them and to place them in a secure place.

The Lord says that just as the rain and snow come down from heaven and water the ground and they do not return but make the earth to bring forth plants and trees that benefit the sower, so is his word that goes forth out of his mouth. It shall not return void but it shall accomplish that which the Lord pleases and it prospers to fulfill the purpose for which it was sent out.

"So shall my word be that goeth forth out of my mouth: it shall not return unto me void, but it shall accomplish that which I please, and it shall prosper in the thing whereto I sent it". (Isaiah 55:11)

There is an assurance for the one who believes in the Lord that he shall go out with joy and be led with peace. There will be heavenly blessings showered on him. (Isaiah 55:12-13). But it should not be misunderstood that the life of a believer on this earth will be like bed of roses. Surely we will have our rewards in heaven.

Jesus has forgiven many with grave sins when they sought him. In Jesus alone is salvation. Seek him while he may be found. Jesus said to the woman of Samaria that he will give living water. (John 4:10)

****

www.ingramcontent.com/pod-product-compliance
Lightning Source LLC
Chambersburg PA
CBHW070637030426
42337CB00020B/4048